Arduino Home Automation Projects

Automate your home using the powerful
Arduino platform

Marco Schwartz

BIRMINGHAM - MUMBAI

Arduino Home Automation Projects

First published: July 2014

Production reference: 1160714

Published by Packt Publishing Ltd.
Livery Place
35 Livery Street
Birmingham B3 2PB, UK.

ISBN 978-1-78398-606-4

www.packtpub.com

Cover image by Pratyush Mohanta (tysoncinematics@gmail.com)

Credits

Author
Marco Schwartz

Reviewers
Santiago Reig Chiva
Charalampos Doukas
Francis Perea

Commissioning Editor
Edward Gordon

Acquisition Editor
Harsha Bharwani

Content Development Editor
Akashdeep Kundu

Technical Editor
Edwin Moses

Copy Editors
Gladson Monteiro
Adithi Shetty

Project Coordinator
Neha Thakur

Proofreaders
Simran Bhogal
Paul Hindle

Indexers
Hemangini Bari
Tejal Soni

Production Coordinators
Aparna Bhagat
Manu Joseph
Conidon Miranda

Cover Work
Conidon Miranda

About the Author

Marco Schwartz is an electrical engineer, entrepreneur, and blogger. He has a Master's degree in Electrical Engineering and Computer Science from Supélec, France, and a Master's degree in Micro Engineering from EPFL, Switzerland.

He has more than 5 years of experience working in the domain of electrical engineering. His interests gravitate around electronics, home automation, the Arduino and Raspberry Pi platforms, open source hardware projects, and 3D printing.

He runs several websites based on Arduino, including the Open Home Automation website that is dedicated to building home automation systems using open source hardware.

He has written another book on home automation and Arduino called *Home Automation with Arduino, CreateSpace*. He has also published a book on how to build Internet of Things projects with Arduino called *Internet of Things with the Arduino Yun, Packt Publishing*.

About the Reviewers

Santiago Reig Chiva received his BEng degree in Electronics Engineering from Universidad de La Rioja (Spain). He is currently finishing his MEng degree in Industrial Engineering from Universidad de Talca (Chile), thanks to a merit-based scholarship.

He has been interested in technology ever since he was a child. He had his first contact with Arduino just before he started university; this got him involved in open source software and hardware.

In his free time, he develops open source projects with Arduino and Python, which he publishes at his personal website, http://kungfulabs.com. He also introduces kids to technology and programming through extracurricular activities and summer camps.

Charalampos Doukas is a researcher and IoT Maker. He started playing with sensors and Arduinos in 2008 while trying to capture and transmit vital signs. He is passionate about combining different hardware systems with software and services using the Internet. He helps in spreading the knowledge about open source software and hardware by organizing sessions at workshops and conferences.

He has built many projects around home monitoring and automation. He is currently contributing hardware nodes for Node-RED and has also authored the book *Building Internet of Things with the Arduino, CreateSpace*.

When he is not playing with sensors and actuators, he manages European research projects at CREATE-NET in Trento, Italy.

Francis Perea is a Professional Education Professor at Consejería de Educación de la Junta de Andalucía in Spain with more than 14 years of experience.

He specializes in system administration, web development, and content management systems. In his spare time, he works as a freelancer and collaborates, among others, with ñ multimedia, a little design studio in Córdoba where he works as a system administrator and the main web developer.

He was also a technical reviewer for *SketchUp 2014 for Architectural Visualization*, *Thomas Bleicher* and *Robin de Jongh*, and *Internet of Things with the Arduino Yún*, *Marco Schwartz*, both by Packt Publishing.

When not sitting in front of a computer or tinkering at his workshop, he can be found running or riding his bike through the tracks and hills or, as a beekeeper, taking care of his bees in Axarquía County where he lives.

I would like to thank my wife, Salomé, and our three kids—Paula, Álvaro, and Javi—for all the support they give me, even though we are all busy. There are no words to express my gratitude to them.

I would also like to thank my colleagues at ñ multimedia and patient students. The need to be at the level they demand is what keeps me going forward.

www.PacktPub.com

Support files, eBooks, discount offers, and more

You might want to visit www.PacktPub.com for support files and downloads related to your book.

Did you know that Packt offers eBook versions of every book published, with PDF and ePub files available? You can upgrade to the eBook version at www.PacktPub.com and as a print book customer, you are entitled to a discount on the eBook copy. Get in touch with us at service@packtpub.com for more details.

At www.PacktPub.com, you can also read a collection of free technical articles, sign up for a range of free newsletters and receive exclusive discounts and offers on Packt books and eBooks.

http://PacktLib.PacktPub.com

Do you need instant solutions to your IT questions? PacktLib is Packt's online digital book library. Here, you can access, read and search across Packt's entire library of books.

Why subscribe?

- Fully searchable across every book published by Packt
- Copy and paste, print and bookmark content
- On demand and accessible via web browser

Free access for Packt account holders

If you have an account with Packt at www.PacktPub.com, you can use this to access PacktLib today and view nine entirely free books. Simply use your login credentials for immediate access.

Table of Contents

Preface

Home automation is a topic that has been around for many years. It includes everything that you can imagine to control and automate your home. The most widely spread example is the alarm system of your home. Motion sensors, contact sensors, and the central device that orchestrates your alarm system are generally the main components of any home automation system.

There are countless devices that are available for home automation. You can buy complete home automation devices from a lot of stores, and even get them installed in your home. However, many of these systems are very expensive, impossible to be customized for your own needs, and have outdated user interfaces.

On the other hand, we have the Arduino platform. Arduino is a platform that you can use to quickly prototype electronic systems. It is now used by millions of people around the world to build more complex systems. It is actually the perfect platform to build home automation systems. Because of the flexibility of the Arduino platform, we are going to see that it is easy to interface with various sensors and actuators that are usually found in many home automation systems. It can also be interfaced with many wireless systems, such as Wi-Fi, Bluetooth, or XBee.

In this book, we are going to see how to build home automation systems with Arduino. We will first build systems based on commercially available Arduino boards. For example, we are going to build a temperature sensor based on Arduino and Bluetooth. We are also going to integrate some of these systems in an Internet of Things perspective, by sending some data directly to a cloud service. Finally, we are also going to see how to hack commercially available devices and build your own home automation systems from scratch.

What this book covers

Chapter 1, Building Wireless XBee Motion Detectors, covers a very common topic in home automation: motion detectors. We are going to build a swarm of motion detectors based on the well-known XBee protocol and Arduino. We are also going to build a server-side interface to monitor the state of the XBee motion detectors.

Chapter 2, Control Lights from Your Phone or Tablet, covers another popular topic in home automation systems: controlling lights remotely. We are going to interface a relay with Arduino and a Wi-Fi chip so that you can control lights in your home not only from your computer, but also from your phone or tablet.

Chapter 3, Measuring the Temperature Using Bluetooth, focuses on measuring temperature and humidity with Arduino, and transmitting the result back to your computer using Bluetooth. We are also going to build a simple interface using Python so that you can access the measurements made by the Arduino and Bluetooth system.

Chapter 4, Weather Station in the Cloud with Xively, teaches you to tackle a very trendy topic: the Internet of Things. We are going to make basic weather measurements on our Arduino board, and then transmit this data via Wi-Fi to the cloud using a service called Xively. Using this service, we'll be able to monitor our data remotely from anywhere in the world.

Chapter 5, Monitor Your Energy Consumption in the Cloud, starts with the use of the same cloud service that was used in *Chapter 4, Weather Station in the Cloud with Xively*. However, in this case, we are going to send energy consumption data to the cloud. This way, you will be able to monitor data directly from the Xively interface.

Chapter 6, Hack a Commercial Home Automation Device, explores the idea of doing things differently. Instead of creating a new home automation system based on Arduino, we are going to hack an existing device so that you can control it from your computer. We are going to build a USB-controlled power switch, so you can control any device right from an interface running on your computer.

Chapter 7, Build Your Own Home Automation System, goes one step further and shows you how to build your own home automation system based on Arduino. We'll cover how to build an Arduino system from scratch, how to design your own PCB, and finally how to design and 3D print a custom case for your project.

What you need for this book

You will need several hardware and software components to create all the projects found in this book. Of course, you can just read the description of the projects and learn this way. However, I really recommend actually doing the projects to really learn about building your own home automation systems based on Arduino.

The hardware components required are detailed at the beginning of each chapter. However, what you will really need for all the projects is an Arduino board. All the projects of the book are based on the Arduino Uno board, which is described in the following URL:

http://arduino.cc/en/Main/arduinoBoardUno

On the software part, there are some software that we will use in all chapters of the book. These are as follows:

- Arduino IDE (http://arduino.cc/en/main/software).

- You will need several libraries. These are detailed in each chapter where they are necessary.

- You will also need a web server running on your computer for some of the projects. I recommend using some software that integrates a web server and a database and that handles all the details for you.

  If you are using Windows, I recommend using EasyPHP. You can download it from the following URL:

  http://www.easyphp.org/

  For OS X, I recommend using MAMP. You can download it from the following URL:

  http://www.mamp.info/

  For Linux, you can follow the instructions given in the following URL to install a web server:

  http://doc.ubuntu-fr.org/lamp

Make sure that the server is running at this point. We are going to use it in several of the projects of this book.

Who this book is for

This book is for all those who are willing to build their own home automation systems based on Arduino. You actually don't need to know anything about the Arduino platform beforehand, since all the projects will be explained step-by-step with clear instructions. The only thing you need in order to follow the projects found in this book is basic knowledge of electronics and programming.

This book is also for electronics hobbyists who want to learn more about doing projects with the Arduino platform. By doing these projects around home automation, you will learn about every aspect of the Arduino platform: how to interface sensors and actuators with Arduino, how to use wireless modules, and even how to build your own Arduino system from scratch.

Finally, this book is also for people willing to learn more about the Internet of Things using Arduino. Nearly all the chapters of the book include wireless communications, and two chapters of the book are dedicated to sending some data to the cloud so that it can be monitored from anywhere.

Conventions

In this book, you will find a number of styles of text that distinguish between different kinds of information. Here are some examples of these styles and an explanation of their meaning.

Code words in text, database table names, folder names, filenames, file extensions, pathnames, dummy URLs, user input, and Twitter handles are shown as follows: "What we are interested in is the `return_value` field, which contains the result of the `digitalRead()` function."

A block of code is set as follows:

```
String data = "";
data = data + timeString + "," + String(temperature) + "," +
   String(humidity) + "," + String(lightLevel);
```

When we wish to draw your attention to a particular part of a code block, the relevant lines or items are set in bold:

```
[default]
if (client) {
  // Process request
  process(client);

  // Close connection and free resources.
  client.stop();
}
```

Any command-line input or output is written as follows:

```
# /digital/7/1
```

New terms and **important words** are shown in bold. Words that you see on the screen, in menus or dialog boxes for example, appear in the text like this: "On Windows, you can find it by navigating to **Control Panel | Network and Internet | View network status and sharing options**."

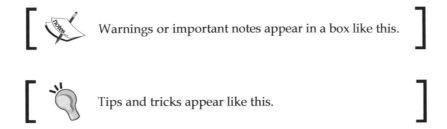

> Warnings or important notes appear in a box like this.

> Tips and tricks appear like this.

Reader feedback

Feedback from our readers is always welcome. Let us know what you think about this book—what you liked or may have disliked. Reader feedback is important for us to develop titles that you really get the most out of.

To send us general feedback, simply send an e-mail to feedback@packtpub.com, and mention the book title via the subject of your message.

If there is a topic that you have expertise in and you are interested in either writing or contributing to a book, see our author guide on www.packtpub.com/authors.

Customer support

Now that you are the proud owner of a Packt book, we have a number of things to help you to get the most from your purchase.

Downloading the example code

You can download the example code files for all Packt books you have purchased from your account at http://www.packtpub.com. If you purchased this book elsewhere, you can visit http://www.packtpub.com/support and register to have the files e-mailed directly to you.

Errata

Although we have taken every care to ensure the accuracy of our content, mistakes do happen. If you find a mistake in one of our books—maybe a mistake in the text or the code—we would be grateful if you would report this to us. By doing so, you can save other readers from frustration and help us improve subsequent versions of this book. If you find any errata, please report them by visiting http://www.packtpub. com/submit-errata, selecting your book, clicking on the **errata submission form** link, and entering the details of your errata. Once your errata are verified, your submission will be accepted and the errata will be uploaded on our website, or added to any list of existing errata, under the Errata section of that title. Any existing errata can be viewed by selecting your title from http://www.packtpub.com/support.

Piracy

Piracy of copyright material on the Internet is an ongoing problem across all media. At Packt, we take the protection of our copyright and licenses very seriously. If you come across any illegal copies of our works, in any form, on the Internet, please provide us with the location address or website name immediately so that we can pursue a remedy.

Please contact us at copyright@packtpub.com with a link to the suspected pirated material.

We appreciate your help in protecting our authors, and our ability to bring you valuable content.

Questions

You can contact us at questions@packtpub.com if you are having a problem with any aspect of the book, and we will do our best to address it.

1

Building Wireless XBee Motion Detectors

In this chapter, we are going to build a project around a very common home automation sensor: a motion sensor. Ever noticed those small modules in white plastic that are in the upper corners in some rooms of people's houses, modules that turn red when you walk in front of them? That's exactly the same thing we are going to do in this project.

However, instead of using proprietary technologies, which is usually the case for these modules, we are going to base our system on Arduino. And for the communication part, we are going to use XBee modules, which are low-power radio modules that are widely used with the Arduino platform. These modules are based on the ZigBee protocol, which is also used in many commercial home automation systems.

Here are the major takeaways that we will see in this chapter:

- First of all, we will list all the hardware and software components that we need for this project. With these components, we will build one motion sensor module composed of an Arduino board, a motion sensor, and one XBee module.

- Then, we will test this first module; the motion sensor will be tested on its own, and we will also test the communication part by sending commands via the serial monitor of the Arduino software.

- Finally, we are going to build a web-based graphical interface that centralizes all the data of our XBee sensors. With a simple interface built on web technologies, you'll be able to instantly see if some motion is detected in your home.

Hardware and software requirements

For this first project, we will need Arduino boards, PIR motion sensors, and some XBee modules and XBee shields, depending on the number of sensors you want to have in your system. For just one sensor, you will need the following components:

- Arduino R3 board (https://www.sparkfun.com/products/11021)
- PIR sensor (http://www.adafruit.com/products/189)
- Series 1 XBee module (https://www.sparkfun.com/products/11215)
- Arduino XBee shield (https://www.sparkfun.com/products/10854)

Note that I added the link to the components I used for this project as a reference, but you can also choose to use other components.

The motion sensor needs to have three pins: two for the power supply and one signal pin. It should also use a 5V voltage level to be compatible with the Arduino Uno board that also operates at 5V.

For the XBee module, I used a Series 1 XBee module, 1mW, with a trace antenna (which means it doesn't require any external antenna). You could also use a module with an external antenna, but you would then have to connect the antenna to the module. I used Series 1 XBee modules for this project as they are easier to use than Series 2, which have functionalities we do not need for this simple project. This module has a range of about 100 meters without obstacles.

You will also need to connect your XBee module to your Arduino board. For that, each of my motion sensor modules will use an Arduino XBee shield from Sparkfun, but you can use other brands as well. It just needs to make the connections between the XBee module and the Arduino board.

Finally, you will need a way to communicate with these XBee modules from your computer. I used another XBee module (also Series 1, 1mW, with a trace antenna) connected to an XBee explorer board from Sparkfun, which is basically a USB interface board where you can plug any XBee module. I used the following components for the module connected to the computer:

- XBee explorer USB (https://www.sparkfun.com/products/8687)
- Series 1 XBee module (https://www.sparkfun.com/products/11215)

On the software side, you need to have the latest version of the Arduino IDE installed on your computer. For this project, the Arduino IDE 1.0.5 was used.

You will also need the aREST library for Arduino. You can find this library at the following link:

```
https://github.com/marcoschwartz/aREST
```

To install the library, extract all the files in a folder named aREST (or create this folder if it doesn't exist yet). Then, place this folder in your /libraries folder inside your main Arduino folder. You will also need to have a web server installed and running on your computer so that you can use the web interface that we are going to develop at the end of this chapter.

To configure your XBee modules, you will also need to have the XCTU software installed. You can find it at the following URL:

```
http://www.digi.com/products/wireless-wired-embedded-solutions/
zigbee-rf-modules/xctu
```

Hardware configuration

The hardware configuration of this project is not really complex. For each motion sensor module you want to build, you'll need to do the following steps. The first one is to plug an XBee module on the XBee shield. Then, you need to plug the shield into your Arduino board, as shown in the following image:

Now, you can connect the motion sensor. It has three pins: VCC (for the positive power supply), GND (which corresponds to the reference voltage level), and SIG (which will turn to a digital HIGH state in case any motion is detected). Connect VCC to the Arduino 5V pin, GND to Arduino GND, and SIG to Arduino pin number 8 (the example code uses pin 8, but you could also use any digital pin). You should end up with something similar to this image:

You will also need to set a jumper correctly on the board so we can upload a sketch. On the XBee shield, you have a little switch close to the XBee module to choose between the XBee module being connected directly to the Arduino board serial interface (which means you can't upload any sketches anymore) or leaving it disconnected. As we need to upload the Arduino sketch first, you need to put this switch to **DLINE**, as shown in this image:

You will also need to connect the XBee explorer board to your computer at this point. Simply insert one XBee module to the board as shown in the following image:

Now that this is done, you can power up everything by connecting the Arduino board and explorer module to your computer via USB cables.

> If you want to use several XBee motion sensors, you will need to repeat the beginning of the procedure for each of them: assemble one Arduino board with an XBee shield, one XBee module, and one motion sensor. However, you only need one USB XBee module connected to your computer if you have many sensors.

Interfacing the PIR sensor with Arduino

First off, you are going to leave XBee aside and simply check if the motion sensor is working correctly. What you will do in the first sketch is print out the readings from the motion sensor on the serial port. This is the complete code for this part that you can just copy and paste in the Arduino IDE:

```
// Simple motion sensor
int sensor_pin = 8;

void setup() {
```

```
    Serial.begin(9600);
}

void loop() {

    // Read sensor data
    int sensor_state = digitalRead(sensor_pin);

    // Print data
    Serial.print("Motion sensor state: ");
    Serial.println(sensor_state);
    delay(100);
}
```

Downloading the example code and colored images

You can download the example code files and colored images
for this Packt book that you have purchased from your account
at http://www.packtpub.com. If you purchased this book
elsewhere, you can visit http://www.packtpub.com/support
and register to have the files e-mailed directly to you.

Let's see what this code does. It starts by declaring the pin on which the sensor is
connected, in our case 8. In the setup() function of the sketch, we initialize the serial
connection with the computer, so we can print out the results on the serial monitor.

Then, in the loop() part of the sketch, we read out the state of the motion sensor
using a simple digitalRead() command, and store that result into a variable. This
state is then simply printed out on the serial port every 100 ms.

You can now upload the sketch to your Arduino board and open the serial monitor.
This is what you should see:

```
Motion sensor state:0
Motion sensor state:1
Motion sensor state:1
Motion sensor state:1
Motion sensor state:0
Motion sensor state:0
```

If you can see the state of the sensor changing when you wave your hand in front of
it, it means that the sensor is working correctly and that you can proceed to the rest
of the project.

Programming an XBee motion detector

You are now going to modify the sketch slightly so that it can transmit the state of the sensor to a central interface running on your computer. However, you not only want to transmit the state of the motion sensor, but also an ID identifying the sensor that is detecting the motion. Programming the detector starts by importing the right libraries:

```
// Libraries
#include <aREST.h>
#include <SPI.h>
```

The aREST library implements a REST API for Arduino. REST stands for REpresentational State Transfer, and is widely used in web applications such as **Software as a Service (SaaS)** applications. In our case, we will use this library to standardize the communication with the central interface that will run on the computer. In this project, the REST commands will be sent over the XBee connection that acts as a serial port from the Arduino point of view.

After importing the libraries, you need to declare the sensor pin and the ID of the module as follows:

```
// Motion sensor pin and ID
int sensor_pin = 8;
String xbee_id = "2";
```

After this, you can create the instance of the aREST library that will handle the requests coming from the graphical interface:

```
// Create aREST instance
aREST rest = aREST();
```

In the setup() function of the sketch, the first step is to start the serial communication. Be careful here, as the speed of the serial object has to be the same as the speed of your XBee modules, which is 9600 bauds by default:

```
// Start Serial
    Serial.begin(9600);
```

You can also set the ID of the module:

```
    // Give name and ID to device
    rest.set_id(xbee_id);
```

Note that if you are configuring more than one sensor, you need to change the ID of each sensor you are configuring. Now, thanks to the aREST **library**, the `loop()` part of the sketch is pretty simple. We simply have to handle the incoming requests from the computer that will come via the XBee serial interface:

```
void loop() {

  // Handle REST calls
  rest.handle(Serial);

}
```

Now, the sketch is ready to be used.

> All the code is available on the GitHub repository of the project:
>
> `https://github.com/openhomeautomation/arduino-home-`
> `automation/tree/master/chapter1`

You can upload the sketch to your Arduino board by making sure that the switch is still set on DLINE. Once this is done, you can test the code locally via the serial monitor of the Arduino IDE. Open the serial monitor, make sure that the serial speed is set to 9600, and type the following:

```
/digital/8/r
```

This is the REST command to read a digital value from pin number 8 and return the value, which is exactly what we want to achieve. You should see the following data being returned, depending on the current state of the sensor:

```
{"return_value": 0, "id": "2", "name": "", "connected": true}
```

What we are interested in is the `return_value` field, which contains the result of the `digitalRead()` function. Try to wave your hand in front of the sensor to see if the return value changes accordingly. Note that the returned data is in the JSON format, which will be really important later when we are going to process this information and display it.

Now that you are sure that the code is working, you can switch over to XBee communication. For that, simply put the switch next to the XBee module to **UART**. Now, the serial port of the Arduino board is directly wired to the XBee module.

By default, all the XBee modules sold are configured on the same **Personal Area Network (PAN)** ID, which is 3332. This means that all the modules will receive data from other modules on the same PAN ID. For experimentation, you can leave it at its default value. However, you might want to change this later, in case your neighbor is, for example, using XBee devices as well.

To continue further, insert the XBee module you want to modify in the USB XBee explorer and open the XCTU XBee tool. Click on the top-left button to add a new device and select the USB explorer serial port. You should get the following screen:

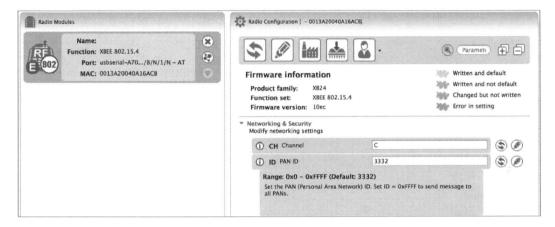

You will then be able to change the PAN ID of your device. To configure all the modules in your network, just repeat the procedure for each XBee module.

Building a graphical interface for your XBee motion detectors

Now that the hardware is completely configured, you can build the server-side code to read data from all your motion sensor modules. For this project, I used two modules only, but you can use more modules for the project.

As for many web applications, our control center for the XBee motion detectors will be built using four different languages: HTML, CSS, JavaScript, and PHP. We are going to use HTML and CSS to design the interface itself, JavaScript to handle the different elements of the interface and make the link with PHP, and finally use PHP to communicate directly with the XBee modules.

The first step is to design the interface. We'll basically have several blocks on our page, one block corresponding to one XBee module. For example, this is the HTML code for the first block:

```
<div class="sensorBlock"><span class="sensorTitle">Sensor 1</span>
    <span class="display" id="display_1"></span>
</div>
```

Now, you can have a look at the JavaScript code that will handle the different elements of the interface. Note that all this code is included inside a dedicated JavaScript file. What we are going to do here is check the value of the sensor at regular intervals via a `digitalRead()` command. To do this, we have to call a PHP file with the correct command as an argument:

```
$.get( "xbee.php", {command: "/digital/8/r"}, function( data ) {
```

The result from the PHP file is some string data formatted in the JSON format. To actually create a usable object from this string, we can use the `parseJSON()` function of jQuery:

```
json_data = jQuery.parseJSON(data);
```

Now, we have a JavaScript object that has the same properties as the data fields inside the JSON container. For example, to get the ID of the sensor module, you can just type:

```
var sensorID = json_data.id;
```

Now that we know which sensor returned some data, we can read the `return_value` field inside the JSON object to know the status of the motion sensor on this module. If this value is equal to `0`, we set the background color of the display block of this sensor to gray. If it is equal to `1`, it means that some motion was detected. If this is the case, we change the background color to orange as follows:

```
if (json_data.return_value == 0){
  $("#display_" + sensorID).css("background-color","gray");
}
else {
  $("#display_" + sensorID).css("background-color","orange");
}
```

Let's now see the details of this PHP file that is called every time. We saw in the JavaScript code that the PHP file also receives an argument called `command`. This variable is retrieved inside the PHP file by:

```
$command = $_GET['command'];
```

Inside this file, we also need to include the php_serial class:

```
include "php_serial.class.php";
```

We also need to declare the right serial port for your XBee explorer device:

```
$serial_port = "/dev/cu.usbserial-A702LF8B";
```

> You will have to change this according to your own settings. To know which serial port the XBee explorer board is using, simply search for devices starting with cu inside your /dev folder if you are using Linux or OS X. If you are using Windows, you will see the list of the serial ports in your Configuration Panel.

You now need to configure the different settings of the serial connection we are about to open with the board:

```
$serial = new phpSerial;
$serial->deviceSet($serial_port);
$serial->confBaudRate(9600);
$serial->confParity("none");
$serial->confCharacterLength(8);
$serial->confStopBits(1);
```

Now, you can actually open the connection:

```
$serial->deviceOpen();
```

We can now send the command and read the answer:

```
$serial->sendMessage($command . "\r");
$answer = $serial->readPort();
```

Now, we close the serial connection:

```
$serial->deviceClose();
```

Finally, we send back the data that was read:

```
echo $answer;
```

We are now ready to test our project. You can of course find all the code for this part on the GitHub repository of the project at the following website:

```
https://github.com/openhomeautomation/arduino-home-automation/tree/
master/chapter1
```

Make sure that your web server is running, and that all the files of the project are placed inside a folder in your web server's main folder. You can now head over to this folder, usually accessible by typing `localhost` in your favorite web browser. Open the HTML file, and you should see something similar to the following screenshot:

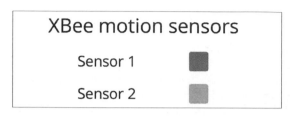

Note that on this example screenshot, the second sensor I had in my system already detected some motion. Now try with your sensors by waving your hand in front of them; you should instantly see that the state of the sensor changes on the interface.

Of course, by modifying the HTML and JavaScript code, you can easily modify this interface to adapt it for more sensors.

Also, be aware that these modules don't need to be connected to your computer directly once the code is loaded onto them. You can just disconnect them from your computer and power them using a simple battery pack (the Arduino Uno board, for example, accepts up to 12 V of power on its jack input).

Note that you can also access this interface from a mobile phone or tablet, just by accessing the `localhost` folder on your computer. Of course, your computer has to be powered (and the web server running) to access the interface.

Summary

Let's now summarize what we did in this first project of the book. We built XBee motion sensors that are based on Arduino, and learned that you can put them wherever you want in your home. They communicate with a central interface where you can see the status of every sensor live.

Of course, we could have used other wireless communication devices for this project, such as Wi-Fi. However, XBee modules are very energy efficient compared to Wi-Fi modules, so it completely makes sense to use XBee for this project, as you might want to power these motion sensors from batteries.

Let's see what the major takeaways of this chapter were. We first chose the components for our project, and built our fist XBee-based motion sensor using Arduino and a PIR motion sensor. We also connected an XBee module to our computer via a USB so it can communicate with the other modules.

Then, we tested our motion sensor module by first testing the PIR sensor connected to the Arduino Uno board. We also tested the sketch at this point that we used to access the board via XBee.

Finally, we built a web-based interface to visualize the information coming from the different XBee motion sensors live. This interface was tested with two modules, but it is made to easily extend to many more XBee modules.

In the next chapter, we are going to tackle another huge field of home automation: controlling lights. And for this project, we won't be using XBee, but we are going to interface Arduino with a Wi-Fi chip to control lights from any mobile device.

2
Control Lights from Your Phone or Tablet

In this chapter, we are going to tackle another very common project in any home automation project: controlling lights. There are many devices that you can buy off the shelves that will give you the ability to control devices in your home, but these devices usually have a high price point. And even if they are wireless, they usually come with a remote control.

In this project, we are going to take another approach and control lights directly from your computer, phone, or tablet, all via Wi-Fi. The following will be the major takeaways from this chapter:

- First, we are going to build the hardware part of our project by connecting a Wi-Fi chip to Arduino and the device we want to control (here, a simple lamp) to a relay module. We'll actually use two relay modules in this project, but this can, of course, be extended to any number you want.

- Then, we are going to write some basic code to test the different parts of the project. We will check that the relay module is functioning properly and that the Wi-Fi chip can indeed be connected to the Wi-Fi network of your home.

- Finally, we'll build a basic graphical interface so that you can control your devices not only from your computer, but also from a mobile device, such as a smartphone or a tablet.

Hardware and software requirements

Let's first see what you will need to create this project. Similar to many other projects of this book, this project is based on the Arduino platform, and we will once again use an Arduino Uno board. Note that an Arduino Mega board will work as well.

Then, you also need some relay modules so that you can control the lamps. A relay is basically an electromechanical switch. They are usually used when you want to command a high voltage device (for example, a lamp plugged into a wall socket) with a much smaller command voltage (for example, the 5V of the Arduino board). For more information on relays, you can visit the following web page:

```
http://en.wikipedia.org/wiki/Relay
```

For this project, I used a 5V relay module from Polulu that can handle up to 250V (thus supporting 110V and 230V devices) and a maximum of 10 A. The following image displays the relay module:

I used two of them, as I want to command two lamps from my Arduino board. Of course, the project will work perfectly fine if you want to add more relays, or just use a single one.

You don't have to get this specific relay module, and you can get one from any of your favorite brands. It just has to have similar characteristics: being compatible with 5V for the command part (so it works with Arduino) and being able to handle the voltage and current of the device you want to control. For example, the module you will see in this project can handle up to 230 V and 10 A, which means the module can handle a device that consumes up to 2300 W of power.

Since we will be using 110 V or 230 V devices with these relays, you will have to take special precautions. Never touch or even go near the relay when it is plugged into the wall power socket via a cable. If possible, hide the relay where other people cannot access it, for example, in a plastic enclosure.

Now, you need a Wi-Fi module. The code of this project is specific for the CC3000 Wi-Fi chip. This chip is widely used in the Arduino community, and you will find a lot of tutorials and resources on the Web that use this specific chip. I used a breakout board from Adafruit that contains this chip. A breakout board is basically a **printed circuit board** (**PCB**) that integrates the chip you are interested in, plus all the extra components that are necessary for the correct operation of the chip. This is an image of the board I used:

Again, you have quite a lot of options when choosing this board. You can pick one from any of your favorite manufacturers. It just needs to integrate the CC3000 Wi-Fi chip and be compatible with 5V voltage levels (which is the case for most CC3000 boards). You can also use an Arduino shield that integrates the CC3000 chip, like the one from Adafruit.

To get more information about this board and how the CC3000 Wi-Fi chip works in general, you can check out the documentation and example of the Adafruit CC3000 library at the following link:

```
https://github.com/adafruit/Adafruit_CC3000_Library
```

You will also need a breadboard and some jumper wires to make all the required hardware connections.

The following is a list of the components that were used in this chapter:

- Arduino Uno R3 (`http://www.adafruit.com/products/50`)
- Polulu 5V relay (`http://www.pololu.com/product/2480`)
- CC3000 Wi-Fi module (`http://www.adafruit.com/products/1469`)
- Breadboard (`http://www.adafruit.com/product/64`)
- Jumper wires (`http://www.adafruit.com/product/759`)

To actually plug the lamp into your relays, you will need some bare male and female power cables. See the hardware configuration section for more details. On the software side, you need to have the latest version of the Arduino IDE installed on your computer. You will also need to install the aREST library for Arduino, which you can find at the following link:

`https://github.com/marcoschwartz/aREST`

To download a repository from GitHub, you can simply click on the **Download ZIP** button. Using the aREST library also requires having the CC3000 chip library, which we will use later in the book. You can find this at the following location on the Web:

`https://github.com/adafruit/Adafruit_CC3000_Library`

You can find the CC3000 mDNS library at the following website:

`https://github.com/adafruit/CC3000_MDNS`

To install a given library, extract all the files in a folder named `aREST`. Then, place this folder in your `/libraries` folder inside your main Arduino folder (or create this folder if it doesn't exist yet).

You will also need to have a web server installed and running on your computer so that you can use the web interface that we are going to develop at the end of this chapter.

Hardware configuration

Let's now see how to connect the different parts of the project. We are first going to take care of connecting all the components to the Arduino board, basically the relay module and the CC3000 Wi-Fi chip. To give you an idea, this is what you should end up with:

To know exactly which wires and pins you have to connect, the following image describes all the connections of the project:

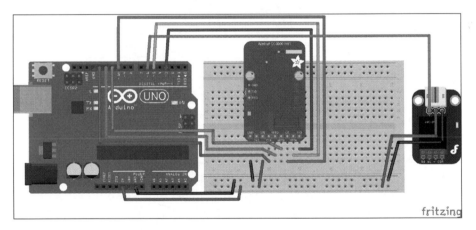

Note that this schematic only displays the connections for one relay module. Let's first see how to connect a single relay module. To get started on the hardware connection, first place the different components next to each other and plug the CC3000 module on the breadboard. We are first going to take care of the power supply part. Connect the ground (GND) pin of the Arduino board to the GND pin of the CC3000 board. Then, connect the Arduino Uno board 5V pin to the Vin pin of the CC3000 board.

Now, let's look at the CC3000 chip. There are quite a few pins to connect to the module, so please be sure to follow the instructions carefully or the module might not work properly. Connect the IRQ pin of the CC3000 board to pin number 3 of the Arduino board, VBAT to pin 5, and CS to pin 10. Then, you need to connect the SPI pins to the Arduino board: MOSI, MISO, and CLK go to pins 11, 12, and 13, respectively.

Then, we'll finish up with the relay module. A relay module has three input pins: VCC, GND, and SIG, which is the signal pin. Simply connect pin number 6 of the Arduino board to the SIG pin of the relay module. Finally, connect GND to the Arduino GND, and the VCC pin to the Arduino 5V.

Now we'll make the connections between the lamp and the relay module. You should have two different cables for that: a male power plug and a female power plug. The following image illustrates the final result you should get:

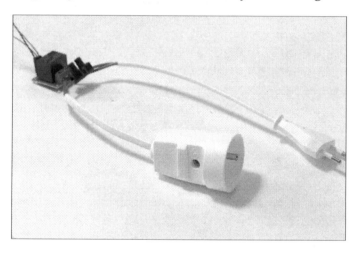

A relay module basically has three output pins: COM (for common pin), NC (for normally closed), and NO (for normally open). What we want is to have the COM pin connected directly to one pin of the power plug, NC not connected, and NO connected to another pin of the power plug.

To connect the relay module to the power cables, take the following steps:

1. First, connect one pin of the female power plug to the COM pin.
2. Then, connect one pin of the male power plug to the NO pin.
3. Finally, connect the two remaining cables together, for example, by using a typical electrical screw terminal.

4. Once this is done, you can go on and connect the project to your lamp. The following schematic summarizes the connections between the relay module and the lamp:

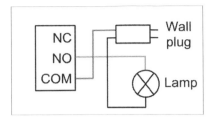

5. Connect the lamp to the female power socket and then connect the male power plug to the power socket in the wall. Of course, you need to repeat this operation for every relay you have in your project. You can simply connect the power supply of each new relay module to the +5V and GND lines on the breadboard, and the SIG pin of the new relay to a free digital pin on the Arduino board.

Testing the relays and Wi-Fi connection

Now that the hardware configuration is complete, we can start writing some code to test our project. We'll first write a simple sketch to test a given relay. Go over to your Arduino IDE and you can start writing some code. The most important parts of the code will be detailed below, and you can find the complete code on the GitHub repository of the project at https://github.com/openhomeautomation/arduino-home-automation/tree/master/chapter2.

The first step is to declare which pin the relay you want to test is connected to:

```
const int relay_pin = 6;
```

We use a `const int` variable here, which is similar to #define but better, since we are sure the constant is of the right type. In the setup() function of the sketch, we need to specify that this pin is a digital output with the pinMode() function:

```
pinMode(relay_pin,OUTPUT);
```

Then, inside the `loop()` function, we are basically going to activate the relay, wait for 5 seconds, switch it off again, wait for 5 seconds again, and repeat the process. This is done with the following piece of code:

```
// Activate relay
digitalWrite(relay_pin, HIGH);

// Wait for 5 seconds
delay(5000);

// Deactivate relay
digitalWrite(relay_pin, LOW);

// Wait for 5 seconds
delay(5000);
```

You can now upload the code to the Arduino board. If you made the right hardware connections, you should now see your lamp switching on and off every 5 seconds. If that's not the case, you need to check your hardware connections, especially between the relay module and Arduino. You should hear the relay click whenever the state of the relay is changing.

Make sure that whenever you touch any part of the project, the power plug is disconnected from the wall socket. There could be a bare cable exposed on your project and it can become very dangerous if you work on your project while it's on.

 Of course, all the code for this first test sketch is available on the GitHub repository of the project at https://github.com/openhomeautomation/arduino-home-automation/tree/master/chapter2, inside the relay_test folder.

We can now work on the next step, which is actually building the final sketch for our project. At this point, we are simply going to test if the CC3000 Wi-Fi chip is working, and check if we can command the relay wirelessly.

We start by declaring the correct libraries for our project:

```
#include <Adafruit_CC3000.h>
#include <SPI.h>
#include <CC3000_MDNS.h>
#include <aREST.h>
```

We also need to specify which pins the CC3000 chip is connected to. If you followed the hardware configuration section, you should have nothing to change here:

```
#define ADAFRUIT_CC3000_IRQ   3
#define ADAFRUIT_CC3000_VBAT  5
#define ADAFRUIT_CC3000_CS    10
```

Then, we have to declare the CC3000 chip instance from the CC3000 library, along with the right pins that we just defined:

```
Adafruit_CC3000 cc3000 = Adafruit_CC3000(ADAFRUIT_CC3000_CS,
  ADAFRUIT_CC3000_IRQ, ADAFRUIT_CC3000_VBAT, SPI_CLOCK_DIV2);
```

Then, there are some parameters you actually need to modify so the chip knows which Wi-Fi network to connect to. You have to enter your Wi-Fi network SSID and password:

```
#define WLAN_SSID       "yourSSID"
#define WLAN_PASS       "yourPassword"
#define WLAN_SECURITY   WLAN_SEC_WPA2
```

Note that you will also have to change your security settings if you are not using WPA2. To get a list of all the possible security settings, you can have a look at the example sketches inside the CC3000 library:

```
// Security can be WLAN_SEC_UNSEC, WLAN_SEC_WEP, WLAN_SEC_WPA
   or WLAN_SEC_WPA2
```

You also need to define a port on which we are going to listen for incoming connections. I used 80, which is quite convenient because you can directly type commands in your browser to access the board:

```
#define LISTEN_PORT         80
```

We'll also need to define the server that will run on the Arduino board and accept incoming connections:

```
Adafruit_CC3000_Server restServer(LISTEN_PORT);
```

We also need to make an instance of the mDNS service, which will be quite useful to access the board without having the IP address of the board:

```
MDNSResponder mdns;
```

Finally, you have to make an instance of the aREST library, so we can handle the requests coming from the outside world:

```
aREST rest = aREST();
```

Inside the setup() function, after initializing the board and connecting to the local Wi-Fi network, you can start the mDNS service. This is where you actually give a name to your Arduino board. Here, we simply call it arduino, which means it will be accessible later using the name arduino.local in your browser:

```
if (!mdns.begin("arduino", cc3000)) {
    while(1); }
```

However, it can be that the mDNS server is not working on your computer. I invite you to check the page of the CC3000 mDNS library for more details. If your computer is not compatible, you will have to know the exact IP address of the CC3000 board. This is done with the following function that will print the IP address whenever the board starts:

```
while (! displayConnectionDetails()) {
    delay(1000); }
```

Before the end of the setup, we still need to start our server running on the Arduino board. This is done with the following piece of code:

```
restServer.begin();
Serial.println(F("Listening for connections..."));
```

Now, in the loop() function of the sketch, we first have to update the mDNS service:

```
mdns.update();
```

And finally, check if any client wants to connect to the Arduino web server, and handle this client using the aREST library if that's the case:

```
Adafruit_CC3000_ClientRef client = restServer.available();
rest.handle(client);
```

And thanks to the aREST library, that's all we have to do! You can now upload the code to the board (make sure that you changed the code with your own SSID and password). When that's done, open the serial monitor, wait for a few seconds, and you should see the following output at the end:

```
Listening for connections...
```

If you can see this message, it means your board is connected to the Wi-Fi network. You should also see the IP address of the board being printed. Write it down, you might need it soon.

You can now close the serial monitor and open your favorite web browser. What we will do first is set the relay pins as outputs, starting with pin number 6. Just type the following command in the URL field of your browser:

```
http://arduino.local/mode/6/o
```

If everything is working fine, you should see the confirmation being printed in your browser:

```
Setting pin D6 to output
```

If that's not the case, don't panic. It could simply be that the mDNS library is not compatible with your computer. Try the same command again with the IP address of your CC3000 board in place of the `arduino.local` alias. For example, type the following command:

```
http://192.168.0.103/mode/6/o
```

You can now do the same for pin number 7, where I connected the second relay when building the project. Now, we'll try to activate the first relay via Wi-Fi. Still present in your browser, type:

```
http://arduino.local/digital/6/1
```

You should instantly hear the relay switching and the lamp being switched on if it's still connected to your Arduino project. You will also have the immediate confirmation inside your browser:

```
Pin D6 set to 1
```

You can also do the same for pin number 7, just to check that the other relay can also be commanded via Wi-Fi. Of course, if you are using more relays or have connected your relays differently, you can test them all at this point just by repeating the procedure we saw in this section.

> Of course, all the code for this section is available on the GitHub repository of the project at the following web page:
>
> https://github.com/openhomeautomation/arduino-home-automation/tree/master/chapter2

Building a graphical interface to control the relays

Although it's good to use commands directly inside your browser to test the project, it's not so convenient to actually use the project for daily use. That's why we are going to build a dedicated interface so that you can control your relays from your computer, just by clicking on some buttons.

Since we'll use web technologies to do so, this interface will also be accessible from your mobile phone or tablet, as long as you are connected to the same Wi-Fi network.

Just as seen in the first chapter of this book, we are going to use a mix of HTML, CSS, JavaScript, and PHP to build the interface. Let's first see the important part of the HTML file. It is basically composed of several blocks, each corresponding to a relay. For each relay, there are two buttons: one to set the relay on and one to set it off. The following is the code which is responsible for that part:

```
<div class="relayBlock"><span class="relayTitle">Relay 1</span>
    <button class="btn btn-block btn-lg btn-primary" type="button"
      id="1" onClick="relayClick(this.id)">On</button>
    <button class="btn btn-block btn-lg btn-danger" type="button"
      id="2" onClick="relayClick(this.id)">Off</button>
</div>
```

To actually make these buttons do something useful, we need to link them to some JavaScript code. This is done inside the JavaScript file. We basically get the ID of the button that was clicked to send the correct command to the system. For example, the button with ID 1 will be linked to the relay connected on pin number 6 and will turn this relay on:

```
if (clicked_id == "1"){
    $.get( "update_relay.php", {
  command: "/digital/6/1"} );
}
```

The same is done for all relays of the system. Of course, depending on the number of relays you have and your hardware configuration, you will need to modify the code in this file.

Let's now see this PHP file, which is called every time we press a button. We saw that a variable named command is passed whenever a button is pressed. Inside the PHP file, we need to get the value of this variable:

```
$command = $_GET['command'];
```

Now that we have the command we want to send, we can build the string that will contain the URL we have to call. That's exactly the same thing we did in the browser when testing the sketch. Note that again, if the mDNS service is not working for you, you will have to enter the IP address of your CC3000 board here. This is how we build the variable containing the URL and command to call:

```
$service_url = 'http://arduino.local'. $command;
```

Now, we can initialize the cURL service that we already used in the first section of the book. This is done with the following piece of code:

```
$curl = curl_init($service_url);
```

After that, we execute the command using the following statement:

```
$curl_response = curl_exec($curl);
```

Then, close the cURL call with the following code:

```
$curl_close($curl);
```

Note that here, we are not really interested with the answer from the Arduino board, so we won't be using it outside of the PHP file.

Testing the graphical interface

It's now time to test the interface. Make sure that the web server is running on your computer. Also, make sure that all the files of the interface are placed inside a folder at the root of your web server. You can go over to this folder in your browser (by typing in `localhost`) and open the HTML file. This is what you should see:

To test the interface, simply try to click on these different buttons. You will see that the lights switch instantly whenever you press the right button. If it doesn't work at this point, there are several things you can check.

The first thing is to check that your web server is running correctly. Also, check that you have entered the right name for your Arduino board (or the right IP address) inside the PHP file. Finally, make sure that your Arduino sketch is working correctly by typing the commands inside your web browser directly. Also, note that at this point, you should also have set the relay pins to be outputs, as we saw in the section where we tested our Arduino sketch.

Of course, all the code for the interface is available on the GitHub repository of the project at the following web page:

```
https://github.com/openhomeautomation/arduino-home-automation/tree/
master/chapter2
```

You can now also go over to your mobile device, smartphone, or tablet, and use this interface. To do so, simply find out the name of your computer on the network. This really varies depending on your operating system, but it is usually in a menu similar to the one called **Network preferences** in your system settings. For example, on OS X, my computer was accessible by the name `macbookpro.local`. On Windows, you can find it by navigating to **Control Panel | Network and Internet | View network status and sharing options**. If you are using Linux, you can simply type the hostname in a terminal.

By entering the name of your computer inside your mobile device, you will be able to directly go to the folder where the interface is stored. You should now be able to use it in the same way you used it on your computer. This is, for example, what it looked like on my smartphone:

Summary

Let's summarize what we did in this chapter. What we did in this project was build a system to wireless command relays from your computer or mobile device. The project works the same as a commercial device that you can buy in any hardware store, but you get the advantage of being able to customize the system for your needs. And you also have the advantage of controlling these devices right from your smartphone, and not from yet another remote control.

Let's see what the major takeaways from this chapter were. First, we chose the components to build our system, including the relay modules to connect with the devices to be controlled. We also chose a Wi-Fi chip so that the project can be connected to your local Wi-Fi network.

Then, we assembled the hardware part of the project. We also connected the desk lamp to the project, so we could control it via Wi-Fi.

We then wrote the Arduino code to test the different components of the project. We tested the relay modules separately, and then we checked if the project can be connected to your local Wi-Fi network.

Finally, we built a web interface, so it's easier to control the different devices connected to the system. Since this interface was built using web standards like HTML and JavaScript, it is accessible from any browser or mobile device.

Of course, it is possible to add more Arduino boards to the project if you want to have relays in two different rooms, for example. To do so, you first have to give a unique name to each board, for example `arduino1.local`, `arduino2.local`, and so on. Then, you will have to change the server-side code accordingly.

3

Measuring the Temperature Using Bluetooth

In this third chapter of the book, we are going to use yet another technology for home automation purposes. We will use a very commonly used technology for sensors, namely, Bluetooth. We are going to interface a Bluetooth module with Arduino, make some measurements using Arduino, and transmit this data back to your computer via Bluetooth. To receive and display the data on your computer, we are going to use the programming language Python.

The following are the major points we will see in this chapter:

- We are first going to select the different hardware components for the project, including the Arduino board, the Bluetooth module, and the temperature and humidity sensor. At this point, we will also install the different software components that are required for the project.

- Then, we will actually build the hardware part of the project. To do so, we'll connect the different components together using a breadboard and some wires.

- Right after the hardware assembly, we are going to build the Arduino sketch for our project. At this point, we will be able to test our hardware to see whether all the connections were made correctly.

- Finally, we are going to build a graphical interface based on Python that will automatically measure the data and display it on your computer, all via the Bluetooth interface.

Hardware and software requirements

Let's first see what we need to build this project. The project is once again based on the Arduino Uno board, but it will also work with other Arduino boards such as Arduino Mega. Due to the differences in the architecture, especially in the behavior of the serial port, some more recent boards such as Arduino Due or Arduino Leonardo might now work with the code that we are going to build in this project.

Then, the other important component of the project is the Bluetooth module. I used the Bluefruit EZ-Link Bluetooth module from Adafruit for this project. It integrates a Bluetooth chip and all the required electronics for the module to work with Arduino. It is really easy to use and interfaces directly with the serial port of your Arduino board.

 You can find documentation on this Bluetooth board at the following URL:

https://learn.adafruit.com/introducing-bluefruit-ez-link

Of course, it should be possible to use other Bluetooth modules for this project. Just make sure that they have a direct serial output/input (usually denoted as TX/RX). If that's the case, they can be interfaced with the Arduino serial port, and you can follow the instructions of this project.

The following image shows the module I used for this project, which is already integrated into the completed project that we are going to build in this chapter:

You will also need a sensor to measure the temperature and humidity. I used a DHT sensor for this project, which is a digital temperature and humidity sensor. Inside the sensor, there are two parts: a thermistor to measure the temperature and a humidity sensor. A chip inside the sensor does all the analog-to-digital conversion. It is really convenient to use with Arduino and comes with a nice Arduino library.

There are actually two versions of this sensor: DHT11 and DHT22, the second one being more precise. You can use the version you want; you'll just have to change one line of the code. Along with the DHT sensor, you will need a 4.7k ohm resistor for the sensor to work correctly. This is necessary to create a pull up on the data line. We will see how to insert this resistor in the next section. You can learn more about these sensors at the following URL:

```
https://learn.adafruit.com/dht
```

You can also use a sensor of your choice, or even two separate sensors. You can use, for example, an analog sensor for the temperature and a digital sensor for humidity; it's completely up to you. You will just need to make sure that these measurements end up in the correct variables in the Arduino sketch.

To make connections between different components, you will also need a breadboard and some jumper wires. You will also need a 10 uF polarized capacitor to program the Arduino board via Bluetooth. Indeed, one of the cool things about this kind of Bluetooth module is that it acts as a serial port just like USB, so you will be able to program your Arduino board wirelessly. A capacitor is needed to do that, as it will be used between the Bluetooth module and the Arduino board to drive the reset pin and set Arduino into the programming mode.

The following is a list of all the components that were used for this project:

- Arduino R3 board (`http://www.adafruit.com/products/50`)
- Bluefruit EZ-Link Bluetooth module (`http://www.adafruit.com/products/1588`)
- DHT11 sensor and resistor (`http://www.adafruit.com/product/386`)
- 10 uF capacitor (`https://www.sparkfun.com/products/523`)
- Breadboard (`http://www.adafruit.com/products/64`)
- Jumper wires (`http://www.adafruit.com/products/758`)

 Because of this last point, you don't actually have to plug the board via USB. You can simply use an external power source, such as a battery, to power the Arduino board.

The following is a list of the software requirements:

- You will need the DHT library for this project, which can be found at `https://github.com/adafruit/DHT-sensor-library`.

  To install a library, you simply need to place the folder into the `/library` folder of your main Arduino folder.

- Finally, you will need to have a working installation of Python 2.7 for this project. It comes already installed on many operating systems, but if this is not the case, you can find it at `https://www.python.org/downloads/`.

- You will also need to get the Python serial library, which is available at `http://pyserial.sourceforge.net/`.

  The instructions to install this library can be found at `http://pyserial.sourceforge.net/pyserial.html#installation`.

- You can also chose to install a Python distribution that already comes preinstalled with pySerial. You can get this from the following web page:

  `https://store.continuum.io/cshop/anaconda/`

 The complete code for this project is available at the GitHub repository that corresponds to this chapter; it is found at the following web page:

`https://github.com/openhomeautomation/arduino-home-automation/tree/master/chapter3`

Hardware configuration

Let's now build our project. We will have to connect the different modules and sensors with Arduino, connect the smaller components (such as a resistor and capacitor), and connect everything together using jumper wires.

To help you out in visualizing the different connections that have to be made, you can have a look at the following image:

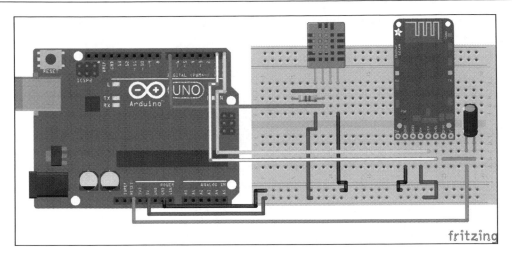

To build our project, let's execute the following steps:

1. The first step is to place the Arduino board next to the breadboard so that you can easily make different connections. You can also place the Bluetooth module at this point. When you are done with placing the components, you should have something similar to the following image:

2. We'll now take care of the connections of the Bluetooth module, starting with the power. You have to connect the GND pin of the Arduino board to one of the blue power rail of the breadboard, which will be the negative rail from now. You can also connect the 5V of the Arduino board to the red power rail, which will be the positive power rail. You can also connect the Bluetooth module to the power at this point. The Vin pin of the Bluetooth module has to be connected to the red power rail, and the GND pin has to be connected to the blue power rail:

3. You can now place the 10uF capacitor between the DTR pin of the Bluetooth module and the RESET pin of the Arduino board. Make sure you have the negative side of the capacitor (marked with a gray line) connected to the Arduino RESET pin.

4. Then, you can place the DHT sensor on the board. We are going to connect the DHT sensor to the power first. The VCC pin (pin 1) of the DHT sensor has to be connected to the red power rail, and the GND pin (pin 4) has to be connected to the blue power rail of the breadboard. The following image shows how it should look at this point:

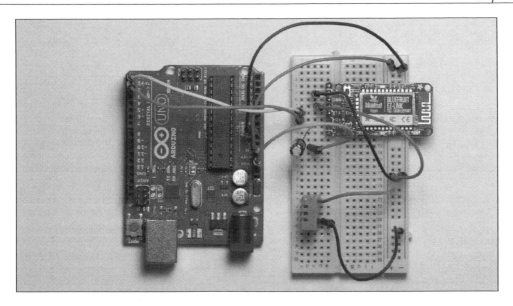

5. Finally, you have to connect the SIG pin (pin 2) of the DHT sensor to the Arduino pin number 7. You also need to connect the 4.7k ohm resistor between the VCC pin of the sensor (pin 1) and the SIG pin.

6. For the Bluetooth module, you will have to connect the TX pin to Arduino's RX pin and the RX pin to the Arduino TX pin.

The following image will give you an idea of what you should end up with:

Creating the Arduino sketch

Let's now build a simple sketch to test our sensor via Bluetooth. We are going to build a sketch so that it measures the temperature and humidity from the DHT sensor when a given command is received on the serial port.

We start by including the DHT library so that we can use the DHT11 sensor:

```
#include "DHT.h"
```

Then, define the sensor's pin and type:

```
#define DHTPIN 7
#define DHTTYPE DHT11
```

Note that if you are using a different DHT sensor, you will need to modify the code here. For example, if you are using a DHT22 sensor, simply type the following:

```
#define DHTTYPE DHT22
```

You will also need to define an instance of the DHT sensor and to send the sensor type and sensor pin as an argument:

```
DHT dht(DHTPIN, DHTTYPE);
```

In the `setup()` function of the sketch, you will have to initialize the DHT sensor's instance and start the serial connection:

```
dht.begin();
Serial.begin(115200);
```

We need to use a speed of 115,200 bauds here instead of the standard 9600 bauds, as it is recommended in the specifications of the Bluetooth module.

Then, in the `loop()` function, we are going to constantly check the status of the serial port to see whether a command was received from the computer:

```
if (Serial.available()) {
```

If that's the case, we will read out the content of this command. This is simply done using the following line of code:

```
byte c = Serial.read ();
```

If we receive a measurement command, simply denoted as m, we proceed further in the sketch:

```
if (c == 'm'){
```

The first thing we do when the measure command is received is to measure the data from the DHT sensor:

```
float h = dht.readHumidity();
float t = dht.readTemperature();
```

Note that if you are using another sensor or two different sensors, this is where you have to do your own measurements.

Then, we want to return some data to the serial port. For this project, we'll use a very simple protocol and return the data in the format temperature, humidity. This is done by printing these values on the serial port:

```
Serial.print(t);
Serial.print(",");
Serial.println(h);
```

This means that if Arduino receives the correct character, the measurements will be returned to the computer via the Bluetooth module.

The complete Arduino sketch is available on the GitHub repository of the project at the following web page:

https://github.com/openhomeautomation/arduino-home-automation/tree/master/chapter3

Testing the temperature and humidity sensor

It's now time to compile the sketch and upload it. To do so, we are going to use the Bluetooth connection. Let's execute the following steps to test the temperature and humidity sensor:

1. Once your project is powered up (either by using a USB cable or an external power source), you can go to the Bluetooth preferences of your operating system. You should see that the Bluetooth module has been detected. Note that the name of this Bluetooth module will change depending on your own module, as shown in the following screenshot:

2. Just click on the pair button (or a similar button depending on your operating system) and the Bluetooth module should be linked to your computer.

3. Now, let's get back to the Arduino IDE. You should now be able to select the Bluetooth module in the serial ports' list. At this point, you can either select the one starting with `tty` or `cu`; it does not matter for testing purposes. Note that depending on your setup, you will see different names being displayed, but always with EZ-Link on it:

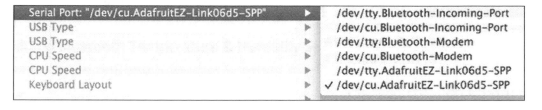

4. You can now upload the sketch to your Arduino board. Simply click on upload as usual, and the sketch should be uploaded to the board. Note that compared to the usual sketch transfer via USB, the Bluetooth connection is much slower.

5. You can now open the serial monitor to test the sketch. Again, you will notice that there is some lag compared to the USB connection, and the serial monitor can take a few seconds to open. Now, simply type in m and this is what you should get:

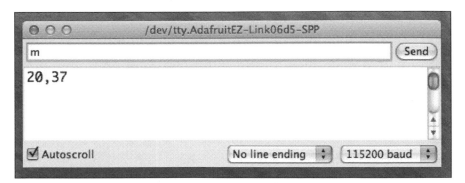

If you can see the measurements being printed out on the serial monitor, it means that the sensor is working correctly. It also means that the project is responding as expected when it receives the signal to measure data.

If you cannot see the measurements at this point, the first step is to check your wiring. Also, make sure that the Bluetooth module is correctly paired with your computer. Usually, you can easily see that information by checking the Bluetooth preferences panel of your operating system again. If the serial interface opens but you can't see that the data is being printed out after you send the measurement command, it means that the problem could have been triggered by the DHT sensor. In this case, make sure that you correctly wired the sensor and inserted the resistor between the signal and the VCC pins.

Measuring the temperature and humidity remotely

Now that the basics of the project are working, we can go further. We clearly don't want to constantly have the serial monitor from the Arduino IDE open and type commands by hand. This is why we need to build a graphical interface on your computer.

In this section, we are going to build a simple graphical interface using Python and the graphical library that comes with it, Tkinter. All the code will simply be contained in a Python file that can be executed later to open the interface.

The first step of the Python code is to import the correct Python modules. Python modules are basically like Arduino libraries; they add additional functions to Python. We need the `time` module, the `serial` module that we installed before, and every other component of the Tkinter module:

```
import time
import serial
from Tkinter import *
```

If you need more information on the Tkinter module, you can visit the official documentation page at `https://wiki.python.org/moin/TkInter`.

We have to set up the serial connection just as we did in the serial monitor of the Arduino IDE. The first step is to set the serial speed and the serial port. Of course, you will have to modify the serial port depending on how it appears on your computer:

```
serial_speed = 115200
serial_port = '/dev/cu.AdafruitEZ-Link06d5-SPP'
```

We can now create the serial instance with the following parameters:

```
ser = serial.Serial(serial_port, serial_speed, timeout=1)
```

The next step is to create the class that will contain our graphical interface:

```
class Application(Frame):
```

Inside this class, there will be several functions to create different elements of the interface. We are not going to look at the details of every single function, but the most important one is the function to send the measurement order to the board:

```
def measure(self):
```

Inside this function, we simply have to send the m command to the serial port to trigger the measurement on the Arduino board. Then, we immediately read the data that will be reflected on the serial port:

```
ser.write("m")
data = ser.readline()
```

After that, we have to check whether the received data is valid. We simply check that it is not empty:

```
if (data != ""):
```

If that's not the case, it means we received a message from the board. Remember that we are going to receive data in the form of `temperature,humidity`. That's why we need to use the `split()` function of Python to separate this data and store it into an array:

```
processed_data = data.split(",")
```

This means that you now have an array where the temperature measurement is stored inside the first cell and the humidity in the second. We can now update the interface accordingly. For example, the `temperature` field is updated with the following piece of code:

```
self.temp_data.set("Temperature: " + str(processed_data[0]))
self.temperature.pack()
```

The same is also done to display humidity. We also want to update the interface automatically. That's why this function is repeated every second. This is done using the following piece of code:

```
self.after(1000,self.measure)
```

Finally, we have to start the application at the end of the Python file. This is done using the following piece of code:

```
root = Tk()
app = Application(master=root)
app.mainloop()
```

> The complete code is available on the GitHub repository of the project at the following web page:
>
> `https://github.com/openhomeautomation/arduino-home-automation/tree/master/chapter3`

You are now ready to test the project. Make sure that the Arduino sketch we developed earlier is loaded onto the board, that the board is powered (via USB or an external power source), and that the Bluetooth module is paired with your computer. You can now simply go to a terminal window, go to the folder where the Python file is located, and type the following:

```
python interface.py
```

This should open the interface and immediately make some measurements from the Arduino board. The following is what you should see on your screen, depending on your operating system:

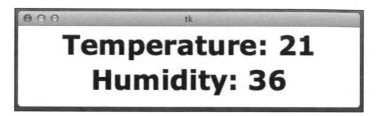

If you can't see the interface at this point, there are several things you can check. First, make sure the Arduino sketch is working just as we tested it in the previous section. Also, make sure that your Python installation is working correctly and that the Python sketch does not produce errors. If you can see some errors that are being displayed inside your terminal, the first step is to use the Python file that is given on the GitHub repository that corresponds to the book. Please also check that all the required libraries are installed such as the Python serial library.

Summary

In this project, we built a Bluetooth- and Arduino-based temperature and humidity sensor. Using this sensor, you can measure data that comes from your Arduino board via Bluetooth and display this data on your computer.

Let's see the major takeaways from this chapter. In the first part of the chapter, we chose the components of this project, including the Bluetooth module and the temperature and humidity sensor. We also downloaded and installed the required software components of the project.

Then, we built the hardware part of the project and made the required connections on the breadboard. We connected the Bluetooth module and the temperature and humidity sensor to the Arduino board.

Then, we spent some time building the main sketch of the project. At the same time, we tested the project by checking whether the Bluetooth connection was actually working. We also checked whether the temperature and humidity sensor was working correctly.

Finally, we used Python to build a simple interface on your computer. Using this interface, we established a connection to the Arduino board via Bluetooth and displayed the measurement data on your computer.

There are also several ways to improve the project. You can easily couple Python and a database, for example MySQL, to automatically log measurements locally on your computer. You can also couple this project, still using Python, with one of the Python-plotting modules to constantly display the measured values on a graph.

In the next chapter, we are going to use Wi-Fi again but for a completely different purpose. This time, we are not going to measure and store data locally, but automatically upload data to a cloud service so that it is stored and displayed there.

4
Weather Station in the Cloud with Xively

Until now, we have only built home automation systems that can be accessed locally. We built XBee motion sensors, controlled lights via Wi-Fi, and also measured temperature and humidity data using Bluetooth. In this chapter, we are going to take another approach to building home automation systems.

We are going to make some measurements on your Arduino board, but send this data to a cloud service called Xively instead of sending these measurements to a local server. Xively is an online platform where you can send data from various devices such as Arduino. We want to send data to Xively so that it can be recorded on their servers, and after that it can be accessed from anywhere in the world through a web browser.

This will be the first project of this book: linking home automation to the "Internet of Things", which is a major trend at the moment. The Internet of Things is this idea of having every device connected on the Web, such as not only computers and smartphones, but also fridges, coffee machines, and so on, so that they can all communicate with each other.

The following are the major takeaways from this chapter:

- First, we are going to interface several sensors with your Arduino board, including temperature and humidity sensors and a light-level sensor. We are also going to use the CC3000 chip again to connect to the Internet.
- Then, we are going to test the different sensors locally to make sure that the hardware is working correctly before doing anything related to the cloud.

- The next step is setting up a Xively account and configuring it. This way, you'll be given your different credentials so that the Arduino board knows where to send data. We are also going to create a dashboard where you will be able to visualize the recorded data.

- Finally, we are going to build the final sketch for your Arduino board and connect to the Internet. The sketch will automatically upload data to Xively at regular intervals. We are also going to visualize this data right on the Xively website and see data coming in in real time.

Hardware and software requirements

Let's first see what components we need for this project. You will need the usual Arduino Uno board. Other boards such as Arduino Mega would work as well, but this project has not been tested with more recent boards such as Arduino Leonardo or Arduino Due.

You will also need a board that hosts the CC3000 Wi-Fi chip. I used the Adafruit CC3000 Wi-Fi board again, but you can also use an Arduino shield that hosts this Wi-Fi chip like the Adafruit CC3000 shield.

 Other boards or shields hosting the same Wi-Fi chip would work as well, but there are no guarantees and you might have to slightly change the code of the project.

For the temperature and humidity measurement, we are going to use a digital sensor, the DHT11. Note that you can also use the DHT22 sensor, which is more precise and works with the same library.

You can also use your own sensor for these measurements, or even two sensors, but you will then have to change the code accordingly. You will also need a 4.7k ohm resistor for the project to work.

For light-level measurements, you will need a photocell (which is simply a resistor that changes its resistance according to the ambient light) and a 10k ohm resistor. Of course, you will need the usual breadboard and jumper wires to make the connections between the different components.

This is a list of the components that are used in this chapter:

- Arduino Uno R3 (http://www.adafruit.com/products/50)
- CC3000 Wi-Fi module (http://www.adafruit.com/products/1469)
- DHT11 sensor and resistor (http://www.adafruit.com/product/386)

- Photocell (`http://www.adafruit.com/product/161`)
- Breadboard (`http://www.adafruit.com/product/64`)
- Jumper wires (`http://www.adafruit.com/product/759`)

On the software side, you need to have the latest version of the Arduino IDE installed on your computer, as well as the DHT library for the DHT11 sensor that will be used in this project. You can find this library at `https://github.com/adafruit/DHT-sensor-library`.

This project also requires the CC3000 chip library. You can find it at `https://github.com/adafruit/Adafruit_CC3000_Library`.

To install a given library, extract all the files in a folder named aREST. Then, place this folder in your /libraries folder inside your main Arduino folder (or create this folder if it doesn't exist yet).

Connecting the different components

In this project, there are basically three things you will have to connect: the CC3000 Wi-Fi chip, the temperature and humidity sensor, and the light sensor.

To know exactly which wires and pins you have to connect, take a look at the following image that describes all the connections of the project:

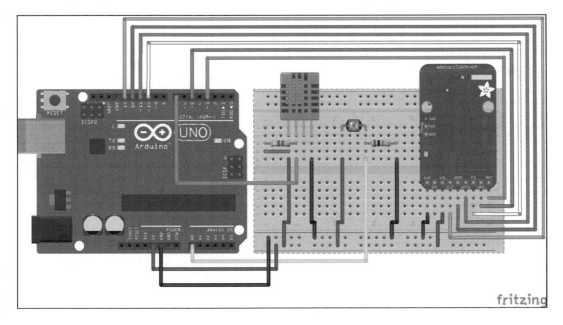

Let's connect the different components by executing the following steps:

1. To get started on the hardware connection, first place the different components next to each other and plug the CC3000 module and the sensors into the breadboard. To reduce the number of wires needed, plug one pin of the photocell with one pin of the 10k ohm resistor. Also, plug the 4.7k ohm resistor between pin number 1 and 2 of the DHT11 sensor, just as shown in the previous image.

2. As we have quite a lot of devices to power, I suggest you first connect the red power rail to the Arduino 5V pin and the blue power rail to the Arduino GND pin.

3. We'll first take care of the sensors. The DHT11 sensor has three pins that have to be connected: two for the power supply and one for the signal. Connect pin number 1 (VCC) to the red power rail, and pin number 4 (GND) to the blue power rail. Finally, connect pin number 2 (signal pin) to Arduino pin number 7.

4. For the photocell, you need to connect the remaining pins of the photocell to the red power rail, and the remaining pins of the resistor to the blue power rail. Finally, connect the common pin to the Arduino pin A0.

5. Now, it's time to work with the CC3000 chip. There are quite a few pins to connect for this module, so please be sure to follow the instructions carefully or the module might not work properly. Connect the IRQ pin of the CC3000 board to pin number 3 of the Arduino board, VBAT to pin 5, and CS to pin 10. Then, you need to connect the SPI pins to the Arduino board: MOSI, MISO, and CLK go to pins 11, 12, and 13, respectively.

6. You can now plug the board to your computer via USB, and you're ready to write your first sketch for this project.

Testing the sensors

Before sending the data from our sensors to the cloud, we'll first make sure these sensors are working correctly. To do this, we are going to make the usual test sketch that will try to read data from the sensors and print this data on the serial monitor.

Let's now go to the Arduino IDE. The Arduino sketch starts by importing the correct library for the DHT sensor. The library is as follows:

```
#include "DHT.h"
```

We also have to declare the variables to store the measurements:

```
int lightLevel;
float humidity;
float temperature;
```

And to define on which pin the DHT sensor is connected, use the following code:

```
#define DHTPIN 7
#define DHTTYPE DHT11
```

We also have to create the instance for the DHT sensor:

```
DHT dht(DHTPIN, DHTTYPE);
```

In the `setup()` function of the sketch, we need to initialize the DHT sensor:

```
dht.begin();
```

Then, start the serial connection:

```
Serial.begin(115200);
```

In the `loop()` function of the sketch, we make the measurements:

```
float temperature = dht.readTemperature();
float humidity = dht.readHumidity();
int lightLevel = analogRead(A0);
```

And print these measurements on the serial port:

```
Serial.print("Temperature: ");
Serial.println(temperature);
Serial.print("Humidity: ");
Serial.println(humidity);
Serial.print("Light level: ");
Serial.println(lightLevel);
Serial.println("");
```

This is repeated every 500 milliseconds:

```
delay(500);
```

> The full code can be found inside the GitHub repository of the project at the following URL:
>
> ```
> https://github.com/openhomeautomation/
> arduino-home-automation/tree/master/chapter4
> ```

You can now upload the code to your Arduino board and open the serial monitor. Make sure that the serial speed is set to 115,200 bauds. You should see the measurement data being printed every 500 milliseconds:

```
Temperature: 23.00
Humidity: 40.00
Light level: 728
```

If that's not the case, you will need to check the hardware connections again. Go through all the connections again, and make sure they are similar to the connections on the schematics.

Setting up your Xively account

Let's now set up your Xively account. We are going to create an account and then configure it so that you can upload data to Xively. At the end, you will have your API key and feed ID that you will have to enter into Arduino later. These two parameters are important for smooth operation of the project. The API key is used to authenticate on the Xively server when we make a request to store data from the Arduino board. As for the feed ID, it will be used by Xively to know on which device the data has to be stored.

We start by creating an account. Go to the main Xively signup page at `https://xively.com/signup/`.

Enter your information on the page and complete the registration process:

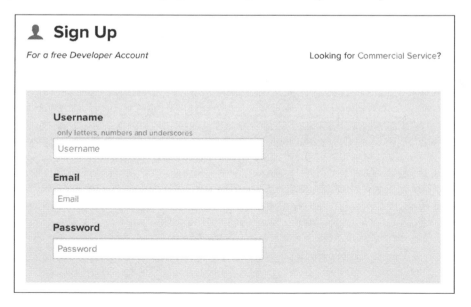

Then, once you are logged in, you will need to create a device. To do so, go to the **Develop** tab and click on **Add Device**. You will be taken to the following screen:

On this page, insert the name of your device, a short description, and set the device as a private device so that only you can access it. Finish up by clicking on **Add Device**.

You will then be able to select it from the list of all the devices you have on your account. On the **Device** page, we now need to create channels for our device that will receive the data from our sensor. Let's create the first one by clicking on **Add channel**:

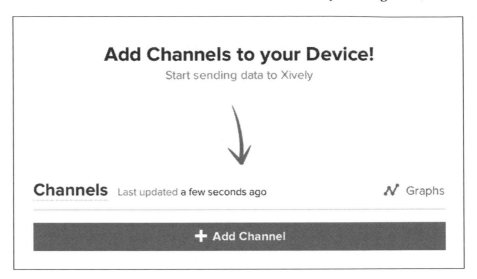

You can then enter data about your channel. The most important aspect is the name of the channel. For example, in this project, I named the channels `Temperature`, `Humidity`, and `Light`. Simply enter the name of each channel and whether you want the unit of the recorded data (but that is optional).

Now, you also need some information about your device and account for the Arduino sketch. You first need to get the feed ID from the top of the page:

On the same page, you will also see an auto-generated API key for this device, as shown in the following screenshot:

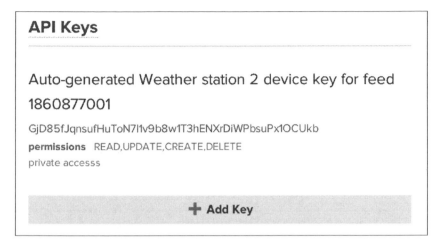

Write this API key down as well; you will need it later.

Building the Arduino sketch

At this point, we have working sensors on our Arduino board, and we also have an account on Xively that is ready to receive some data. We are now going to write the sketch that will connect to your Wi-Fi network and upload data automatically to your Xively account.

We are now going to write down the code in the Arduino IDE. We start by including the correct libraries as shown:

```
#include <Adafruit_CC3000.h>
#include <SPI.h>
#include "DHT.h"
```

Then, just as in *Chapter 2, Control Lights from Your Phone or Tablet*, we need to define on which pins the CC3000 board is connected:

```
#define ADAFRUIT_CC3000_IRQ    3
#define ADAFRUIT_CC3000_VBAT   5
#define ADAFRUIT_CC3000_CS     10
```

And define the pin and type of the DHT sensor:

```
#define DHTPIN 7
#define DHTTYPE DHT11
```

We can now create the instance of the CC3000 chip:

```
Adafruit_CC3000 cc3000 = Adafruit_CC3000(ADAFRUIT_CC3000_CS,
   ADAFRUIT_CC3000_IRQ, ADAFRUIT_CC3000_VBAT, SPI_CLOCK_DIV2);
```

Now, you will have a few things to modify in the sketch. The first couple of things are the SSID and password of your Wi-Fi network:

```
#define WLAN_SSID        "yourSSID"
#define WLAN_PASS        "yourPassword"
```

Now, you need to enter some information concerning Xively that we got earlier in this chapter. Modify these lines so that you use your own API key and feed ID:

```
#define WEBSITE  "api.xively.com"
#define API_key
   "GFSM8c7f83E0MMta3FkGAwzVktkzXNN6kXhoRBV8QN1WmkiZ"
#define feedID  "1628598268"
```

Once this is done, we can move to the `setup()` function of the sketch. We start by initializing the CC3000 chip:

```
Serial.println(F("\nInitializing..."));
if (!cc3000.begin())
{
  Serial.println(F("Couldn't begin()! Check your wiring?"));
  while(1);
}
```

Then, in the `loop()` function of the sketch, we start by connecting to your local Wi-Fi network:

```
cc3000.connectToAP(WLAN_SSID, WLAN_PASS, WLAN_SECURITY);
```

We also define the IP address of the Xively website, so that the CC3000 chip knows where it has to connect:

```
uint32_t ip = cc3000.IP2U32(216,52,233,120);
```

It's now time to do the measurements. This is similar to what we saw in the first sketch where we tested the different sensors:

```
float temperature = dht.readTemperature();
float humidity = dht.readHumidity();
int lightLevel = analogRead(A0);
```

Now comes the most complicated part, so bear with me. In order to upload data to Xively, we need to follow a given format so that Xively servers understand what we want to send. This is all defined in the Xively API's documentation, which you can find on the following Xively website:

```
https://xively.com/dev/docs/api/
```

In our case, we need to format the data in the JSON format by including all measurements in a field called `datastreams`. This is the result inside the Arduino sketch, where we put everything in a string variable called `data`:

```
String data = "";
data = data + "\n" + "{\"version\":\"1.0.0\",\"datastreams\" :
  [ {\"id\" : \"Temperature\",\"current_value\" : \"" +
  String((int)temperature) + "\"}," + "{\"id\" :
  \"Light\",\"current_value\" : \"" + String(lightLevel) + "\"},"
  + "{\"id\" : \"Humidity\",\"current_value\" : \"" +
  String((int)humidity) + "\"}]}";
length = data.length();
```

From the preceding code, we also get the length of the data string, which will be used when we transmit data to the Xively servers. Then, we can connect to the Xively server:

```
Adafruit_CC3000_Client client = cc3000.connectTCP(ip, 80);
```

When the sketch is connected to Xively, we can send the data. This will be done by executing several `print()` functions using the `client` instance. To do so, we will use a `PUT` request on the feed ID that we defined before, so the server knows we want to send the JSON data. This is the result in terms of the code inside the Arduino sketch:

```
client.println("PUT /v2/feeds/" + String(feedID) + ".json HTTP/1.1");
client.println("Host: api.xively.com");
client.println("X-ApiKey: " + String(API_key));
client.println("Content-Length: " + String(length));
client.print("Connection: close");
client.println();
client.print(data);
client.println();
```

After the data is sent, we need to read the answer coming from the Xively server before we can continue:

```
while (client.available()) {
  char c = client.read();
  Serial.print(c);
}
```

Finally, in order to save power, we disconnect from the local Wi-Fi network every time:

```
cc3000.disconnect();
```

And we repeat the process every 10 seconds:

```
delay(10000);
```

 The full code can be found inside the GitHub repository of the project at the following URL:

```
https://github.com/openhomeautomation/
arduino-home-automation/tree/master/chapter4
```

Log in and display data on Xively

It's now time to test the project. You can upload the code to the Arduino board and open the serial monitor. You should see that the sketch is connected to the Web and uploading data to Xively. You should also see the answer from the server being displayed in the serial monitor, as follows:

```
HTTP/1.1 200 OK

Date: Wed, 07 May 2014 08:48:05 GMT

Content-Type: application/json; charset=utf-8

Content-Length: 0

Connection: close

X-Request-Id: aedcb75d10ea1556813941846bdaded812904bb4

Cache-Control: max-age=0

Vary: Accept-Encoding
```

If you can see this HTTP/1.1 200 OK code, it means that the transfer was successful. If this is not the case, check that you really have the same sketch as on the GitHub repository, and that you entered your information (Wi-Fi and Xively keys) correctly. Also, make sure that the CC3000 chip is correctly wired.

Let's now check the device's page on Xively. Go again to the **Device** page and you should see the following:

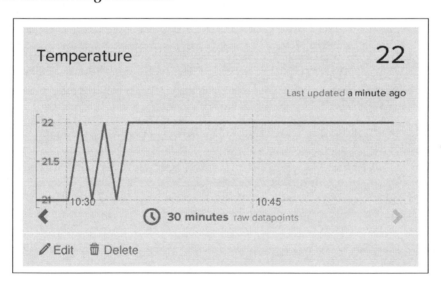

By clicking on the **Graphs** button, you should also be able to see the plots of the data that are being measured. For example, for the temperature, you see the data plot shown in the following screenshot:

The nice thing about this is that the data is measured, sent, and stored continuously on the Xively service. It doesn't depend on your own computer being on or off, so there is an added layer of security and convenience compared to having your own server recording data in your home.

Summary

Let's summarize what we did in this project. We built a simple weather station based on Arduino that can automatically upload data to the Web using the Xively web service. Compared to the approach we used in the previous chapters, this approach allows building autonomous systems that automatically send data to a remote service that stores data in the cloud. This means that your data is safe in the cloud and can be accessed from anywhere in the world; you just need an Internet connection and your Xively account name and password.

Let's see what the major takeaways from this chapter were. First, we built our project around a temperature and humidity sensor, a light-level sensor, and the CC3000 Wi-Fi chip. We assembled everything around an Arduino board and a breadboard for the connections. Then, we wrote a simple Arduino sketch to make sure that we made the correct hardware connections.

After that, we went to our web browser and created an account on the Xively web service. Inside the account, we create a new device to host the measurements coming from our project, and also a set of channels that will receive the individual measurements, for example, the temperature or the light level. We also got a feed ID and an API key that were necessary for our Arduino board to know where to send the data.

Finally, we wrote the final Arduino sketch to upload data to Xively. We tested the sketch to make sure that Xively was receiving data correctly, and also checked on the device's dashboard on Xively that the data was correctly received.

In the next chapter of the book, we are going to take the same principles and apply them to another domain of home automation: energy monitoring. We are going to build a current and power sensor that will automatically send power consumption data to the Web, so you can monitor your energy consumption online.

5
Monitor Your Energy Consumption in the Cloud

In this chapter, we are going to build on what we learned in *Chapter 4, Weather Station in the Cloud with Xively*, and this time, we'll send energy consumption data to the cloud. We are going to interface a current sensor to Arduino and plug a device like a lamp to the project so that you can continuously measure the current and power produced by this device. Then, using the CC3000 Wi-Fi chip, we are going to send this data to Xively so that it can be monitored on the Web.

The following will be the major points we will see in this chapter:

- First, we will interface the different components to the Arduino board. This will consist of connecting the current sensor to the Arduino board as well as the device we want to measure the current from. We'll also connect the CC3000 Wi-Fi to the project so that it can send data to Xively.

- Then, we will build a simple sketch to measure the current locally. This will confirm that the hardware connections of the project were correctly made.

- We will also configure the Xively account so that it can accept the measurements that result from this project.

- Finally, we will build the final sketch that will send data to Xively. Also, we will check the Xively server to confirm that we can indeed follow the energy consumption of the device in real time.

Hardware and software requirements

First, let's look at the components we will need in this project. Just as in the previous chapter, you will need an Arduino Uno board and a board with the CC3000 Wi-Fi chip. For more information on how to choose these two boards, please refer to the previous chapter.

Then, you will need a current sensor. I used a ITead Studio breakout board that hosts the AC712 current sensor. This sensor is an analog sensor that returns a signal that is proportional to the measured current. Later in this chapter, we are going to learn how to calculate the measured current from the output's voltage. You can find more information on how this sensor works inside the datasheet of the sensor at https://www.sparkfun.com/datasheets/BreakoutBoards/0712.pdf.

The following is an image of the board that I used:

You can see in the preceding image that the board has three pins: G for ground, V for VCC, and S for signal, which will deliver the output voltage that is proportional to the measured current.

You should be able to use other suppliers for this sensor, such as Adafruit, SparkFun, or SeeedStudio. Just make sure the sensor board you are using is compatible with the 5V voltage level of the Arduino board.

You will also need two power cables with standard power plugs (one male and one female) to connect a device to your project and to connect the project to a power socket on the wall. Of course, you should use a power plug according to the standard of the country you are living in. For this project, I used standard 230V European power plugs. The power cable in the following image is the same cable I used in *Chapter 2, Control Lights from Your Phone or Tablet*:

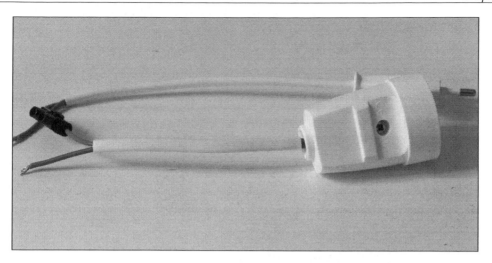

To create some tests with the project, you will also need a device to test. I made the test with a typical 30W desk lamp, but you can choose the AC device of your choice.

> The current sensor is made to measure high currents, so don't take a small AC device or the current readings might be incorrect.
>
> However, on some boards that host the ACS712 current sensor, you have the possibility to change the sensitivity of the current's measurement. So, you might be able to measure lower currents and powers depending on the board you are using.

The following are the hardware requirements:

- Arduino Uno (https://www.adafruit.com/product/50)
- Adafruit CC3000 breakout board (https://www.adafruit.com/product/1469)
- ACS712 module (http://imall.iteadstudio.com/im120710011.html)
- Breadboard (https://www.adafruit.com/product/64)
- Jumper wires (https://www.adafruit.com/products/758)

On the software side, you need to have the latest version of the Arduino IDE installed on your computer as well as the CC3000 chip library:

https://github.com/adafruit/Adafruit_CC3000_Library

To install a given library, extract all the files in a folder named aREST. Then, place this folder in your /libraries folder inside your main Arduino folder (or create this folder if it doesn't exist yet).

You will also need to have an account on Xively. Please refer to the previous chapter for the procedure on how to create an account there.

Making hardware connections

It's now time to make the hardware connections of the project. You need to connect three things: the CC3000 Wi-Fi chip to the Arduino board, the current sensor to the Arduino board, and the power cables to the current sensor.

Because we have several devices to power, I suggest that you should first connect the red power rail to the Arduino 5V pin and the blue power rail to the Arduino GND pin.

There are quite a few pins to connect for CC3000; therefore, follow the instructions carefully so that the module can work correctly. First, connect the IRQ pin of the CC3000 board to pin number 3 of the Arduino board, VBAT to Arduino pin 5, and CS to Arduino pin 10. After that, you need to connect the remaining SPI pins to the Arduino board. The pins called MOSI, MISO, and CLK go to Arduino pins 11, 12, and 13, in this precise order.

The current sensor is quite easy to connect. Connect the V pin to the red power rail, the G pin to the blue power rail, and the S pin to the analog pin A0. The following image shows what the system should look like at this point:

The following schematic figure summarizes the different connections so far:

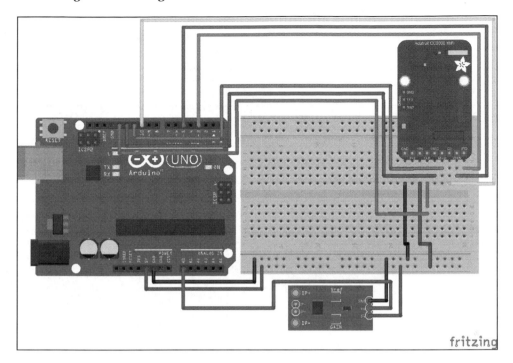

Now, you can connect the power cables to the current sensor so you can connect a device to the system:

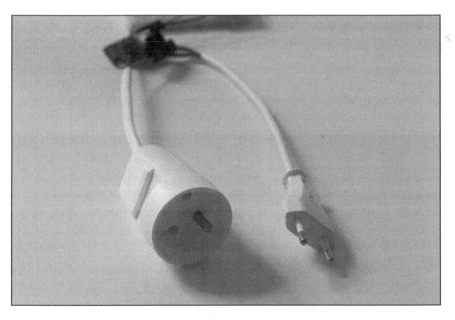

Let's take a closer look at the connections:

The idea is to have two wires of the power cables connected together (via a black connector, as shown in the preceding image), and the other two connected to the current sensor board. This way, the current sensor will sense the current going into the wires. The following schematic diagram illustrates the different connections for this part:

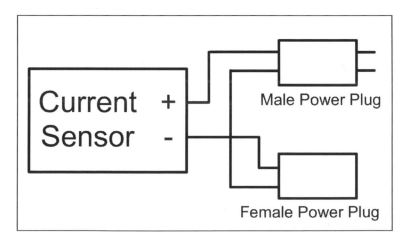

Testing the project

We can now write a simple test for the project, just to see if the hardware connections are correct. We are going to write the code inside the Arduino IDE. Note that this section explains the code for testing the project, and that can you find the complete code in the GitHub repository of the project.

The code starts by defining the pin of the current sensor:

```
#define CURRENT_SENSOR A0
```

We then define the different variables that are necessary for the test. Here, we are going to measure the current and the power. Note that we don't measure the voltage of the device, so you will have to define it yourself depending on your country:

```
float amplitude_current;
float effective_value;
float effective_voltage = 230; // Set voltage to 230V (Europe) or 110V
(US)
float effective_power;
float zero_sensor;
```

Then, in the `setup()` function of the sketch, we need to get the zero value of the sensor. As we have an analog sensor, we need to know what the sensor is reading when no current is flowing:

```
zero_sensor = getSensorValue();
Serial.print("Zero point sensor: ");
Serial.println(zero_sensor);
Serial.println("");
```

Let's now look at the details of this function that measures the value from the sensor. As it's an analog sensor, we need to average the readings over several measurements to get a stable measurement. For this project, the value is averaged over 100 measurements. This is done by the following function:

```
float getSensorValue()
{
  int sensorValue;
  float avgSensor = 0;
  int nb_measurements = 100;
  for (int i = 0; i < nb_measurements; i++) {
    sensorValue = analogRead(CURRENT_SENSOR);
    avgSensor = avgSensor + float(sensorValue);
  }
  avgSensor = avgSensor/float(nb_measurements);
  return avgSensor;
}
```

Inside the `loop()` function, we also measure the value that comes from the sensor using the same function:

```
float sensor_value = getSensorValue();
Serial.print("Sensor value: ");
Serial.println(sensor_value);
```

We can then calculate the value of the effective current, which is given by the datasheet of the ACS712 current sensor:

```
amplitude_current=(float)(
    sensor_value-zero_sensor)/1024*5/185*1000000;
effective_value=amplitude_current/1.414;
```

After this, we print the value of the current, the effective current, and also calculate the effective power:

```
Serial.println("Current amplitude (in mA): ");
Serial.println(amplitude_current,1);
Serial.println("Current effective value (in mA)");
Serial.println(effective_value,1);
Serial.println("Effective power (in W): ");
Serial.println(abs(effective_value*effective_voltage/1000),1);
Serial.println("");
```

We repeat this every 500 ms:

```
delay(500);
```

 The code for this part can be found on the GitHub repository of the book on the following web page:

```
https://github.com/openhomeautomation/arduino-
home-automation/tree/master/chapter5
```

You can now test the sketch. Please make sure that the device connected to the project is completely off, so the initial zero current measurement can be done correctly by the Arduino board. Upload the code to your Arduino board and open the serial monitor. The following is what you should see:

Current amplitude (in mA):

0.8

Current effectivate value (in mA)

0.6

Effective power (in W):

0.1

You can also try to connect the device to your project now, turn it on, and launch the sketch again. You should see the power measurement changing instantly:

```
Current amplitude (in mA):
17.8
Current effectivate value (in mA)
12.6
Effective power (in W):
28.9
```

Configuring your Xively account

Let's now configure your Xively account for this project. At this point, you should already have an account. If not, please create one by following the procedure found in the previous chapter. It starts by creating a new device, as shown in the following screenshot:

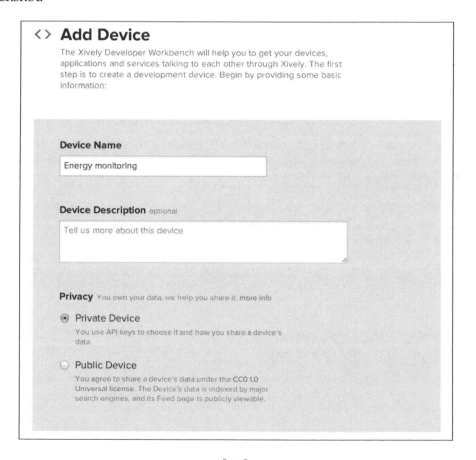

Then, inside this new device, you will have to create two new channels: one for the current and one for the power. I simply call them *power* and *current*:

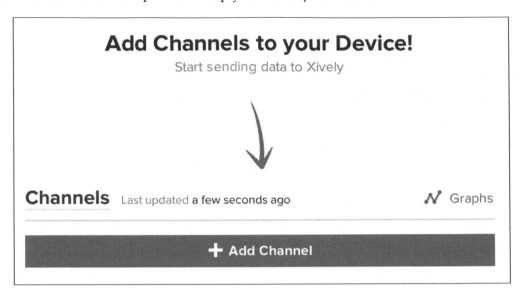

For the power channel, for example, you can even set the right unit (Watts) as shown in the following screenshot:

You should now see the power channel being displayed on the page:

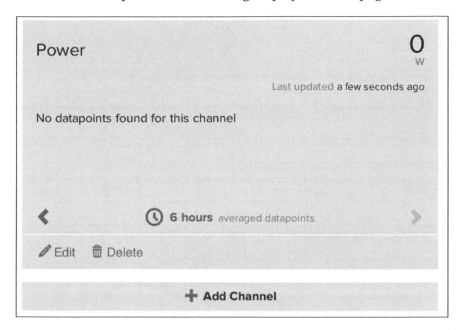

Do the same for the current channel, and you are done. Simply write down the device feed ID and the API key of the device in a note on your computer or on a piece on paper; you'll need them soon.

Sending power consumption data to Xively

Let's now build the sketch that will upload the power measurement data to Xively. The sketch is based on a test sketch, so I will only detail the new parts. We will now go through the most important parts of the code for this section. To get the complete code, please refer to the GitHub repository of this chapter.

It starts by importing the correct libraries:

```
#include <Adafruit_CC3000.h>
#include <SPI.h>
```

We then need to define the pins of the CC3000 chip:

```
#define ADAFRUIT_CC3000_IRQ    3
#define ADAFRUIT_CC3000_VBAT   5
#define ADAFRUIT_CC3000_CS     10
```

After that, we need to declare the CC3000 instance:

```
Adafruit_CC3000 cc3000 = Adafruit_CC3000(ADAFRUIT_CC3000_CS,
  ADAFRUIT_CC3000_IRQ, ADAFRUIT_CC3000_VBAT, SPI_CLOCK_DIV2);
```

Now, this is the part where you need to enter your information. First, you enter the SSID and the password of your local Wi-Fi network:

```
#define WLAN_SSID       "yourSSID"
#define WLAN_PASS       "yourPassword"
#define WLAN_SECURITY   WLAN_SEC_WPA2
```

We now have to enter the API key and the feed ID of your Xively device:

```
#define API_key  "yourAPIKey"
#define feedID   "yourFeedID"
```

In the `setup()` part of the sketch, we need to start the CC3000 chip:

```
if (!cc3000.begin())
{
  Serial.println(F("Couldn't begin()! Check your wiring?"));
  while(1);
}
```

In the `loop()` function of the sketch, we need to connect the CC3000 chip to your network:

```
cc3000.connectToAP(WLAN_SSID, WLAN_PASS, WLAN_SECURITY);
```

Then, we define the IP of the Xively server:

```
uint32_t ip = cc3000.IP2U32(216,52,233,120);
```

Then, we need to format the data. This is all defined inside the Xively documentation; that said, you have to format data inside a JSON container:

```
int length = 0;
String data = "";
data = data + "\n" + "{\"version\":\"1.0.0\",\"datastreams\" : [
  {\"id\" : \"Current\",\"current_value\" : \"" +
  String((int)effective_value) + "\"}," + "{\"id\" :
  \"Power\",\"current_value\" : \"" + String((int)effective_power)
  + "\"}]}";
Serial.println(data);
length = data.length();
```

Once we have the data formatted in a string, we can send it to the Xively server along with the API key:

```
Adafruit_CC3000_Client client = cc3000.connectTCP(ip, 80);
if (client.connected()) {
  Serial.println("Connected!");
  client.println("PUT /v2/feeds/" + String(feedID) + ".json
    HTTP/1.1");
  client.println("Host: api.xively.com");
  client.println("X-ApiKey: " + String(API_key));
  client.println("Content-Length: " + String(length));
  client.print("Connection: close");
  client.println();
  client.print(data);
  client.println();
}
```

After the data is sent, we read back the data that comes from the Xively server:

```
while (client.connected()) {
  while (client.available()) {
    char c = client.read();
    Serial.print(c);
  }
}
```

Then, we disconnect the chip from the local network:

```
cc3000.disconnect();
```

We repeat the procedure every 10 seconds:

```
delay(10000);
```

It's now time to test the sketch.

> The code for this part can be found on the GitHub repository of the book on the following web page:
>
> https://github.com/openhomeautomation/arduino-home-automation/tree/master/chapter5

You can upload the sketch to your Arduino board and open the serial monitor. You should see that the sketch is connecting to the Wi-Fi network, sending data to Xively, and getting the confirmation message from the server.

You can also check whether the data was correctly received on the device page on Xively, as shown in the following screenshot:

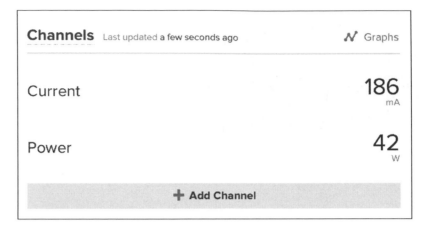

Summary

In this chapter, we built a cloud-connected energy-monitoring device based on Arduino. We connected a current sensor and a Wi-Fi chip to Arduino and built a sketch that allowed data to be sent directly to the Xively platform. This way, the energy consumption data is continuously stored on Xively servers and can be monitored in real time.

So far, we used ready-to-use Arduino boards and modules. However, in the next chapter, we are going to learn the basics of how to build your own home automation devices based on Arduino.

6

Hack a Commercial Home Automation Device

In the previous chapters, we used Arduino boards and other components to build home automation systems from scratch. In this chapter, we are going to take another approach to building home automation systems.

We will take a basic power switch that you can easily buy off the shelf in stores and hack it by inserting an Arduino system inside it. This way, we are going to build a USB-controlled power switch based on Arduino.

The following will be the major takeaways from this chapter:

- First, we are going to see how to choose the device to hack, and which components you will need to hack the device. We are also going to take care of the different software modules needed.

- Then, we will open up the device to hack and replace most of what is inside with an Arduino board and a relay module.

- We will then upload some code to the Arduino board to check if the hardware is working correctly. At this stage, we are already going to command the device remotely from the Arduino IDE.

- Finally, we are going to build a web-based interface to control the device directly from your web browser.

Hardware and software requirements

This project is based on hacking a commercial device to control light directly from your computer via USB. However, the goal is really to teach you how to hack your own device, so the device that you are going to hack doesn't matter that much. Therefore, mentioning a specific brand or product is irrelevant.

 Since this chapter is about hacking a device that uses dangerous voltages such as 110V or 230V, it should be considered only as an informational source and not be used as such in your home for safety reasons. Indeed, there is no way to be sure that the device will continue working properly in the long term once installed in your home.

Also, make sure to never touch the inside of the device when it is under operation and make sure that no cables are coming out of the plastic enclosure.

What you want first is a device that integrates a plug that's controllable remotely. For example, I chose a pack of four identical devices that can be controlled via a small radio remote. Each of these devices is basically an on/off switch that can be controlled by a relay located inside the device.

These devices were very cheap ($9.90 for the four devices) and are perfect to hack as they can be easily opened up. The following image shows such a device:

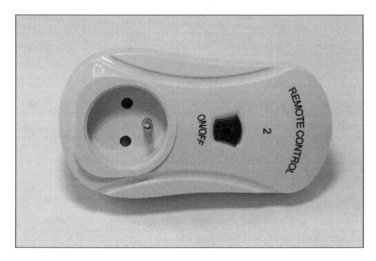

You can take any similar device, the most important thing being that the device is somehow controllable from an electronic system such as a remote control. This is important as we will later insert a relay inside the enclosure to control the switch. Mechanical controllable switches (for example, with only an on/off button on it and no electronics inside) won't work for this project.

Then, you need something to insert inside the device we are going to hack. We first need the "brain" of the system, which is going to be an Arduino board. The problem was that the device I chose for this project was too small to put an Arduino Uno board inside it.

I therefore had to use a smaller Arduino board. I chose to use boards from TinyCircuits, which are some of the smallest Arduino boards available. I used a microcontroller, USB, and prototype board that you can find at `http://tiny-circuits.com/`.

The following is an image of the Arduino boards I used to hack the device:

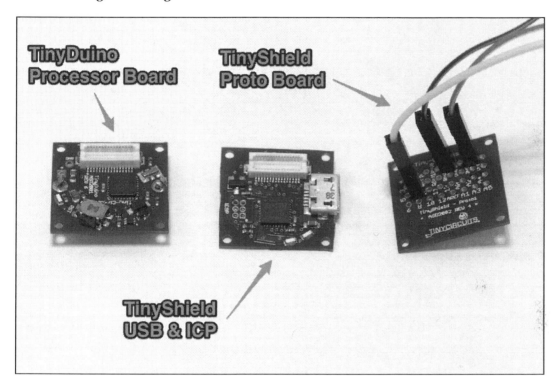

Of course, you can use any other small Arduino boards such as Arduino Micro. You can also use an Arduino Mini for this project. Any basic Arduino board that will fit into the device you want to hack will work.

Then, you will need a relay module to control the plug. I used a 5V Polulu relay module, the same that we used in *Chapter 2, Control Lights from Your Phone or Tablet*:

This is a list of the parts used for this chapter:

- TinyDuino processor board (`https://tiny-circuits.com/shop/ tinyduino-processor-board/`)
- TinyShield USB & ICP (`https://tiny-circuits.com/shop/usb_icp_ tinyshield/`)
- TinyShield proto board (`https://tiny-circuits.com/shop/tinyshield- proto-board-1/`)
- Polulu 5V relay module (`http://www.pololu.com/product/2480`)

On the software side, you need to have the latest version of the Arduino IDE installed on your computer as well as the aREST library for Arduino, which you can find at the following link:

`https://github.com/marcoschwartz/aREST`

You can install the library by simply extracting the library folder in your Arduino `/libraries` folder (you will have to create this folder if it doesn't exist yet).

You will also need to have a web server installed and running on your computer so that we can use the web interface that we are going to develop at the end of the chapter.

Hardware configuration

The first step is to actually open the device you want to hack. The device I used included a lot of electronics inside that I simply removed (we won't need these components anymore), leaving just the important parts: the power plug on both sides of the device and two cables going to both parts of the plug:

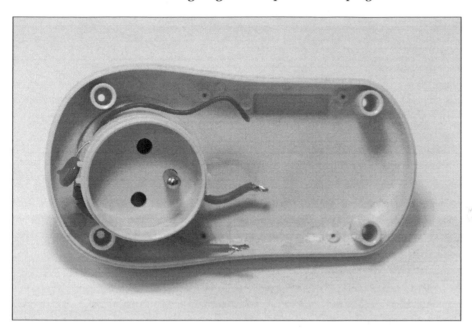

These two cables will have to be connected together if we want to get some current to flow into the device that is plugged into the hacked device. To do so and control the plug from the Arduino board, you need to insert the relay module now.

Basically, a relay has three output pins: a common pin named **COM**, a pin that's **normally closed** (**NC**), and another pin that's **normally open** (**NO**). Normally closed means that this pin is connected to the COM pin of the relay when no voltage is applied to the input of the relay. On the other hand, normally open means that this pin is disconnected when no input is applied to the relay.

You need to connect one of the red cables going to the plug to the COM pin of the relay, and the other one to the NO pin of the relay so that the circuit closes when we signal the relay. The following image shows the device at this step:

Then, you need to insert the Arduino board into the device and connect the relay module to the Arduino board. The connections to the Arduino board are really easy: connect the VCC pin of the relay module to the Arduino +5V pin, the GND pin to the Arduino GND, and the SIG pin to the Arduino pin 7. This is shown in the following screenshot:

Now, you can plug a USB cable into your Arduino board so that you can control it from your computer. I also made a small hole in the device that I hacked so that the USB cable can fit nicely when the device is closed. You can now close the device.

With the device I used, this is how it looked at the end:

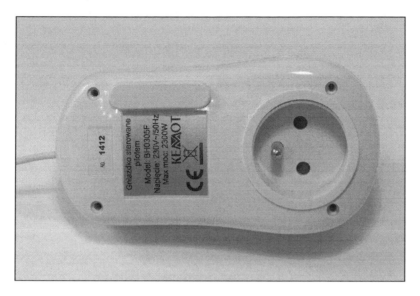

You are now ready to write some Arduino code and test the device that you just hacked!

Controlling the device from your computer

We are now going to build the Arduino sketch we will use to control the relay remotely. This will be based again on the aREST library that will help us handle the request sent from your computer.

This Arduino sketch starts by including the required libraries as follows:

```
#include <SPI.h>
#include <aREST.h>
```

Then, we can create the aREST instance:

```
// Create aREST instance
aREST rest = aREST();
```

Then, in the `setup()` function of the sketch, we simply start the serial connection so that we can access the board later:

```
void setup(void)
{
  // Start Serial
  Serial.begin(9600);

}
```

Next, we can handle the requests coming on the serial port by using the following code:

```
void loop() {

  // Handle REST calls
  rest.handle(Serial);

}
```

 Now, we can actually test the device you just hacked. Note that the code for this part is available on the GitHub repository of the project at the following location:

`https://github.com/openhomeautomation/arduino-home-automation/tree/master/chapter6`

Plug the device into the wall and plug a device inside to test it. For example, I used a simple 30W desk lamp to test my project.

Upload the code for the Arduino board and open the serial monitor inside the Arduino IDE. Make sure the serial speed is set to 9600, and type:

/mode/7/o

This should set the pin number 7 as an output. You should be greeted by the following message:

`Setting pin D7 to output`

You can now switch the relay with:

/digital/7/1

You should hear the relay click and see the device you are trying to control turn on. You should also have the following confirmation on the serial monitor:

```
Pin D7 set to 1
```

If this doesn't work, the first thing to check is the connections inside the device you hacked. Disconnect it first from the power plug in the wall and open it again. Make sure that everything is wired correctly according to the previous section.

You can also test the relay independently by plugging the SIG pin in a 5V pin to see if it's working. Finally, also make sure that the serial speed matches with the speed defined in the Arduino sketch.

Building a graphical interface

However, it's not convenient to control the hacked device from the serial monitor. We are now going to build a simple interface to control this device. The interface will be really basic and include two buttons: one to set the relay on and the other to set the relay off.

The interface is based on HTML for the interface itself, JavaScript to handle the commands, and PHP to interface with the Arduino board. This interface is very similar to the one we developed in *Chapter 2, Control Lights from Your Phone or Tablet.*

The following code will be a walkthrough of the different pieces of the interface. All the files have to be located inside the same folder at the root of your web server folder. You can find the complete code for this part inside the GitHub repository of the book.

Let's first see the HTML file that contains the interface itself. Inside the HTML file, the following is the code for a button:

```
<button class="btn btn-block btn-lg btn-primary" type="button"
    id="1" onClick="buttonClick(this.id)">On</button>
```

Inside the JavaScript file, we first define the communication type and the serial port. This is where you need to change the value of the target to set it to your own serial port. To know which port you need to select, simply go to the **Tools** menu of your Arduino IDE:

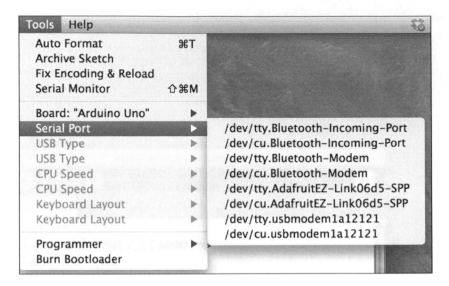

Inside this JavaScript file, this is the code you need to modify:

```
var target = '/dev/cu.usbserial-A102JJ6G';
var type = 'serial';
```

When the window is first loaded, we need to first set the relay pin as an output. This is done using a `get` command inside the JavaScript file:

```
window.onload = function() {
  $.get( "command.php", {target: target, type: type,
  command: "/mode/7/o"} );
}
```

The buttons call a function called `buttonClick` and pass their ID as an argument to this function. For example, this is the code for the ON button:

```
if (clicked_id == "1"){
  $.get( "command.php", {target: target, type: type,
  command: "/digital/7/1"} );
}
```

You can see that all these commands call a PHP file. This file is responsible for interfacing with the Arduino board. The file starts by receiving the different arguments coming from the interface:

```php
$type = $_GET['type'];
$target = $_GET['target'];
$command = $_GET['command'];
```

Since we'll always use serial communications via the USB port in this project, I will only provide details for the part responsible for serial communications. We assign the target to the `serial_port` variable:

```php
$serial_port = $target;
```

Now, we can define the different parameters of the serial connection with the Arduino board:

```php
$serial = new phpSerial;
$serial->deviceSet($serial_port);
$serial->confBaudRate(9600);
$serial->confParity("none");
$serial->confCharacterLength(8);
$serial->confStopBits(1);
```

Now, open the connection:

```php
$serial->deviceOpen();
```

We can then send the following command:

```php
$serial->sendMessage($command . "\r");
  $answer = $serial->readPort();
```

And read the answer (that we won't use in this project):

```php
if ($answer == "") {echo "{\"connected\": false}";}
    else {echo $answer;}
```

The code for this part is available on the GitHub repository of the project at the following location:

```
https://github.com/openhomeautomation/arduino-home-
automation/tree/master/chapter6
```

It's now time to test the interface. Please make sure that all the files of the interface are placed inside a folder on your web server folder, and that the web server is running.

You can now open the HTML file inside the interface folder (usually by typing http://localhost in your web browser), and this is what you should see:

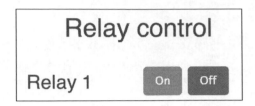

Now, try to click on the ON button. You should instantly hear the relay switching, and see the lamp that is connected to the hacked device turn on.

If it doesn't work at this stage, there are several things to check. The first thing is to make sure that the web server is running on your computer. Also, make sure that you access the HTML file via the localhost folder, and not directly by clicking on the file in your file explorer. Finally, check that the hardware is working correctly by trying to send the commands directly in the Arduino IDE.

You can also get some help on this project by posting your question on the official Arduino forum at http://forum.arduino.cc/.

You can also find similar projects and get help on this chapter at the Open Home Automation blog at http://www.openhomeautomation.net/blog.

Summary

In this chapter, we hacked a commercial device to control a light directly from your computer. We replaced the internal electronics of the device to insert an Arduino board and a relay. This gives us the flexibility of an Arduino-based system with the nice case that came along with the commercial device. After hacking the device, it can then be controlled directly from the web browser of your computer.

Let's see what the major takeaways of this chapter were. In the first part of the chapter, we chose the different components required for the project, including the device to be hacked. We also chose a small Arduino board and a relay module.

Then, we opened up the device to be hacked and inserted the components we chose in the first part of the project.

We then wrote the Arduino sketch to control the device by sending commands on the serial port. We tested this sketch by trying to switch the relay on and off.

Finally, we built a web-based interface to control the hacked device from your web browser.

In the next chapter, we are going to go even further and see how to build our own devices from scratch. We are going to build a low-power Arduino system that can last for years on a simple battery!

7
Build Your Own Home Automation System

So far in this book, we have used only already-assembled Arduino boards and interfaced them with different sensors and modules to build home automation projects. In the previous chapter, we changed things a bit and hacked a commercial device using Arduino.

However, in this last chapter of the book, we are going to take things further and build our own system for home automation. As an example, I will take the design and fabrication of a very simple low-power Arduino board. This board can then be used for home automation projects such as battery-powered motion sensors.

Note that the goal of this last chapter of the book is really to give you a step-by-step method to build your own home automation systems. Therefore, you should not focus on the specific example that is developed in this chapter, but more on the overall methodology to design your own systems.

The following will be the major takeaways from this chapter:

- First, we will choose the required hardware components for the project and install a library dedicated to low-power applications.
- Then, we are going to build a prototype of our custom home automation system on a breadboard to make sure it works correctly. We are also going to test the low-power Arduino library to make sure the board will be power efficient.
- In the next part of the chapter, we will move from the prototyping stage to actually making our own boards. We'll see how to use PCB design software so that you can make your own PCB and then send it to a manufacturer to be built.
- Finally, we are going to see how to make a 3D-printed case for your home automation system and fabricate it.

Hardware and software requirements

Let's first see what components are needed for this project. As an example in this chapter, I will use a project I have previously worked on, which is a low-power Arduino board. This board has just the bare minimum of components to be usable. This way, no power is wasted on components that are not necessary when the system is operating, such as LEDs, a USB interface, and so on. This board can then be used in very low-power applications such as motion sensors based on XBee.

The most important component in this project will be the microcontroller itself. The microcontroller is at the heart of all Arduino boards. It is the component that we program every time we write a new sketch.

I based my design on the Arduino Uno board design, so I used the same Atmel ATmega328 controller as the Arduino Uno board. For this project, you will need one of these microcontrollers, which are sold separately. Please make sure that you are buying one with the Arduino bootloader so that you can directly upload the Arduino code to the microcontroller.

You will also need several smaller components to make the microcontroller work. You will need one 10 uF capacitor, two 22 pF capacitors, one 10k ohm resistor, one 220 ohm resistor, one green LED, and one 16 MHz crystal clock.

You will also need a battery to power up the project. I used a battery pack that can contain two AA batteries (1.5V each) to power the project. You can use the battery of your choice by keeping in mind that the official documentation for this chip says that the voltage should be between 1.8V and 5.5V. However, I really recommend using at least 3 V to power the project.

To program the microcontroller, you will need an external programmer because the project does not integrate a programmer. Instead of using a dedicated programmer, I simply used an Arduino Uno board for this task.

Finally, you will need a breadboard and some jumper cables to make the connections between the different components of the project.

This is the list of all the parts that were used for this project:

- ATmega328 microcontroller with Arduino bootloader (https://www.sparkfun.com/products/10524)
- 10 uF capacitor (https://www.sparkfun.com/products/746)
- 2 x 22 pF capacitors (https://www.sparkfun.com/products/8571)
- 10k ohm resistor (https://www.sparkfun.com/products/8374)
- 220 or 330 ohm resistor (https://www.sparkfun.com/products/8377)
- Green LED (https://www.sparkfun.com/products/9650)
- 16 MHz crystal clock (https://www.sparkfun.com/products/536)
- 2 x 1.5V AA batteries (https://www.sparkfun.com/products/9100)
- Breadboard (https://www.sparkfun.com/products/12002)
- Male/female jumper wires (https://www.sparkfun.com/products/8431)

On the software side, you will need to download the JeeLib Arduino library to enable low-power operation of your system:

https://github.com/jcw/jeelib

To install an Arduino library, simply place the library folder in the /libraries folder of the main Arduino folder.

You will also need to download EAGLE to design your own **printed circuit board (PCB)** for this project. You can download it from the following link:

http://www.cadsoftusa.com/download-eagle/

To design your own 3D-printed case, you can use OpenSCAD, which is a free design tool. You can find it at the following address:

http://www.openscad.org/

Building an Arduino system from scratch

Let's now see how to build an Arduino system on a breadboard using the components we chose.

There are several components to assemble, so the best thing to do is follow the instructions from the following schematic diagram that summarizes all the connections you have to make:

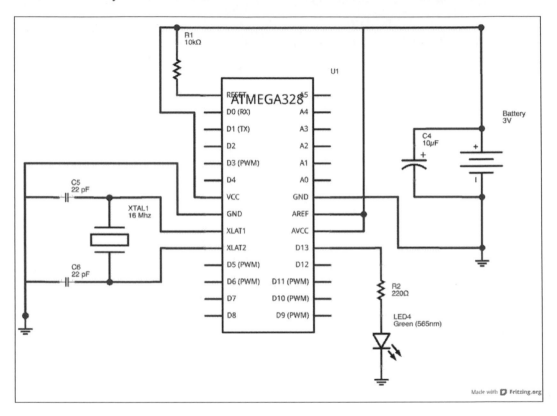

I recommend putting the Arduino microcontroller (ATmega328) first in the middle of the breadboard so you can add the different components around it. This schematic illustrates the placement of the different components:

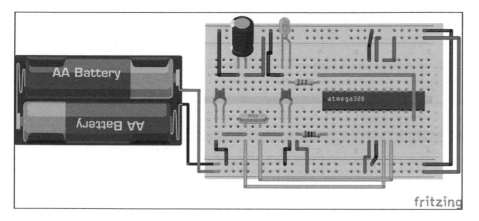

The following image shows a fully assembled system with the battery pack:

We can now test the project, just to see if it is working correctly. To do so, we are going to make the LED flash with the **Blink** sketch that comes with the Arduino IDE.

Testing the Arduino system

It's time now to test the Arduino system. Let's do it in the following way:

- First, take off the chip and place it on the Arduino Uno board, which has to be connected to your computer. To remove the chip from the breadboard or the Arduino Uno board, you can simply use your fingernails or the edge of a knife. Of course, make sure that there is no power flowing through the chip whenever you remove it from a board.

- Load the Blink sketch that comes with the Arduino IDE and upload the code to the board. You should see that the onboard LED is going on and off continuously.

- Now, disconnect the board from your computer and remove the microcontroller. Put it back on the breadboard and connect the power with the battery pack. You should see that the LED inserted on the breadboard is going on and off.

If that doesn't work, there are several things you can check. First, make sure that you correctly wired the different parts of the project according to the schematics. Then, make sure that the microcontroller has been programmed correctly by checking that the onboard LED of the Arduino Uno board is blinking.

Now, we can also make a test with the JeeLib library to put the Arduino controller in a deep sleep mode when it is not active. Indeed, without specifying anything in the code, the Arduino microcontroller will consume power even if it is not doing anything. We need to declare specific commands in the code to put Arduino into a low-power sleep mode.

Let's now see the code for this part. We are going to see the most important elements of the code. You can find the complete code in the GitHub repository of this chapter.

This sketch starts by including the JeeLib library as follows:

```
#include <JeeLib.h>
```

To make sure that the Arduino microcontroller is active, we will also make the LED blink. However, between each change of state of the LED, we will put the microcontroller in a deep sleep mode. We first have to define the pin of the LED we want to control:

```
int led_pin = 13;
```

We also have to start the watchdog, which is necessary to put Arduino in the sleep mode:

```
ISR(WDT_vect) { Sleepy::watchdogEvent(); }
```

In the `loop()` function of the sketch, we switch the LED on and off, but the important part here is that we use a special function to introduce some delay:

```
Sleepy::loseSomeTime(5000);
```

The difference with the `delay()` function of Arduino is that the Arduino controller is put in the sleep mode during this time, whereas with the `delay()` function, the chip just waits.

> The code for this part can be found inside the GitHub repository of the project at the following link:
>
> https://github.com/openhomeautomation/arduino-home-automation/tree/master/chapter7

I performed some measurements to show you the difference with and without the library. Without the use of the library, the system was using 6.7 mA when the LED was off. With the use of the library, it was only consuming 43 uA, which is a 150x improvement over the first case.

This means that for a system which is not active most of the time (such as a temperature sensor or a motion sensor), it can work for years without changing the battery!

Designing a PCB for your home automation system

So far in this chapter, we have learned how to prototype an Arduino-based system on a breadboard. We are now going to see how to take an idea from the prototype we built on a breadboard and build our own board from it.

The first step is to design the board on your computer. To do so, I used software called EAGLE, which is widely used to design Arduino-based systems. You can download EAGLE by going to the following page:

http://www.cadsoftusa.com/download-eagle/

The first thing you have to do is open the software and create a new schematic. This will take you to a new blank window similar to what is shown in the following screenshot, where you will create your schematics:

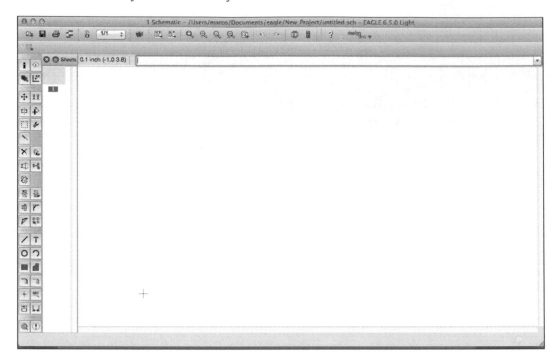

In this section of the chapter, I want to show you how to build your own board and not build the exact same board I used as an example.

Therefore, I will give you an overview of how to build a board in EAGLE. What you should focus on at this stage is really how to use the most important commands of the software.

The first thing we are going to do is create the schematics of our project. This means choosing the components (called parts) that we want for our project, placing them on the screen, and connecting them together via wires.

The important command you are going to need now is the one to place a part, which is located on the left-hand side menu. Once you click on this icon, you will be taken to a menu where you can select the parts you want to use in your project, as shown in the following screenshot:

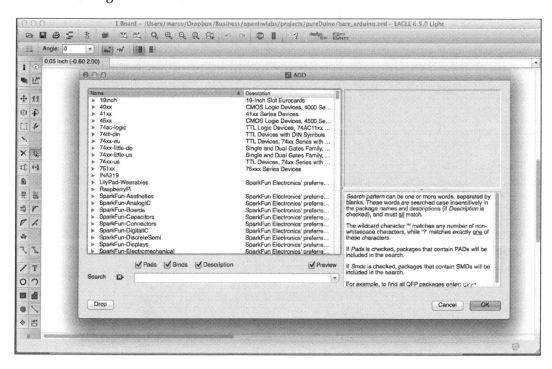

In this menu, you can search for parts you want to use in your project. Whenever you click on a part and click on **OK**, you will be able to place it on the main screen of your project.

You will also need to draw connections between the different parts of the system. This can be done using the Net function, which you will also find on the left menu.

I placed and connected all the components that I had in the previous section of the project. I also added some connectors (to get access to the pins of the microcontroller, like on the Arduino Uno board) to interface the Arduino controller with the outside world, and also a connector for the battery.

The following is the result I had on my screen:

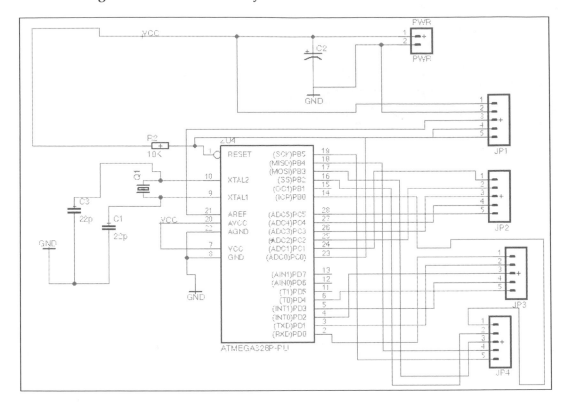

From here, you will be able to do the second step in PCB design: the layout. This is the actual physical representation of your board that will be sent to the manufacturer. You can click on the **Layout** button on the top menu and EAGLE will ask you if you want to generate the layout automatically. Click on **Yes**, and you should see the following screen:

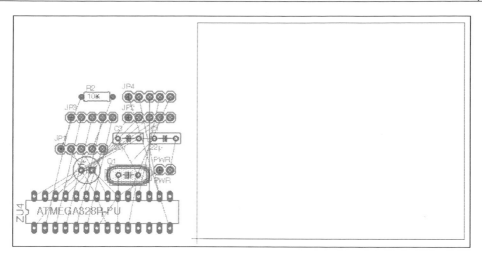

From here, your job is to place the different components (that we chose in the previous step when creating the schematic) on the board, arrange them as you want, and route the board. Routing refers to connecting the different components together on the board using copper traces. This can be done automatically by using the auto-routing functionality of EAGLE. You can see that EAGLE already indicates which components are connected together by displaying thin lines between their pins.

For my example board, I placed all the components first in order to use the least amount of space possible on the board while keeping some space for traces on the board. This is displayed in the following screenshot:

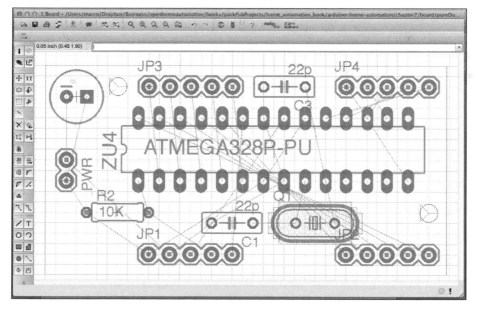

I then used the auto-routing function of EAGLE to automatically connect all the components on the board according to the schematic, as shown in the following screenshot:

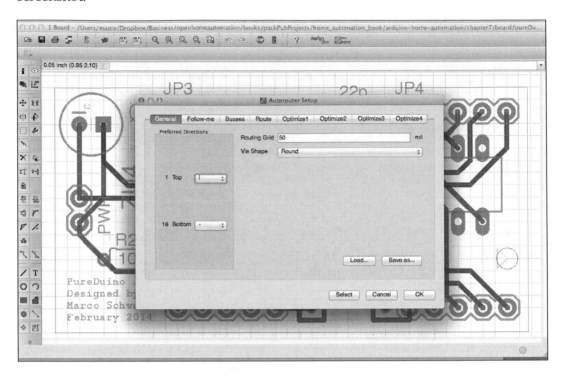

I also inserted two holes so that the board can be mounted on a case. Finally, I inserted some text in the bottom-left corner of the board. This can be done easily using the integrated Text tool that you can also find inside the menu on the left.

The following is the final result in EAGLE:

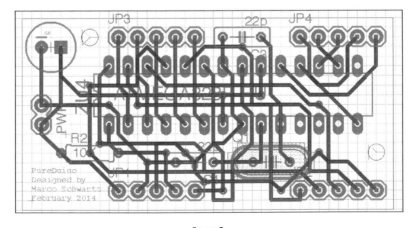

You can see that the Arduino controller is located in the middle of the board, surrounded by the IO pins and components that are necessary for the Arduino operation.

> The code for this part can be found inside the GitHub repository of the project at the following link:
>
> https://github.com/openhomeautomation/arduino-home-automation/tree/master/chapter7

Fabricating the board

When the design step is over, it is time to fabricate the board, order the components, and build it. In this section, we are going to see how to do each of these steps.

For the first step, I usually use the services of OSH Park to build my boards in a small series. It's cheap, fast, and you can send your EAGLE design files directly without having to convert them to another format. You can also use the services from other manufacturers, such as Seeedstudio or Iteadstudio. The link to access the manufacturing services of OSH Park is as follows:

https://oshpark.com/

From the main page, it is really easy to get your board fabricated. You just have to upload your EAGLE board file and the website will automatically analyze it. You will then be taken to the following confirmation page:

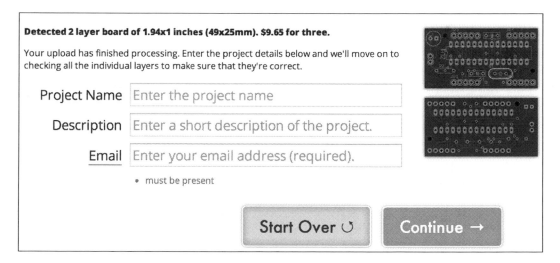

You will then be asked to enter some more details, and you will be able to order and pay for your board. About two weeks later, you will receive it in your mail.

For the second step, which is ordering the necessary components, I recommend using Newark. They have all the components required for the board I used as an example. The link is as follows:

```
http://www.newark.com/
```

You have, of course, many alternatives to Newark. You can also use websites such as Mouser, Digikey, Farnell, or SparkFun.

On the Newark website, you can easily find the components you need with the main search field, as shown in the following screenshot:

When you receive the board and components, you can assemble them using a fine soldering iron. For my board, after assembling it, I repeated the same process I used in the previous section. I first programmed the controller using an Arduino Uno board, and then put the controller back on my custom board for testing.

Designing and 3D printing a case for your home automation project

The third step in designing your own home automation system is to design a custom case for your product. This was a really costly process in the past, as you needed to find a manufacturer for your product and generally produce several thousands of units to have a good price for each unit produced.

Fortunately, 3D printing changed all that. We can now prototype individual systems at a very low cost using this technology. In this section, we are going to see how to make the 3D design of a simple case for our Arduino system. We are also going to see how to send it to a manufacturer so that it can be 3D printed.

And to do so, we are going to use software called OpenSCAD. This is an open source design software where you can actually write code to make your designs. This is perfect if you are not a designer but more of a coder, and it also allows you to make parametric designs that can easily be modified and shared. You can download OpenSCAD from the following URL:

```
http://www.openscad.org/
```

When you open a new project in OpenSCAD, the following is what you should get:

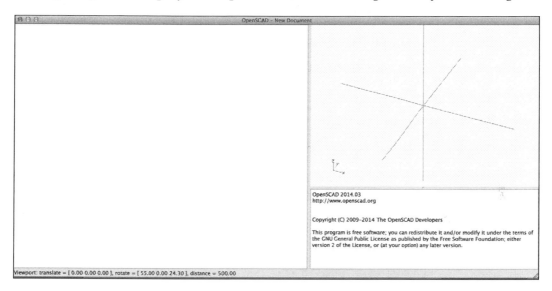

You can see that there are mainly three parts in the OpenSCAD window. There is some space for code on the left, a 3D view of the object on the right, and a window in the bottom-right corner to print out information about the project.

For example, to make a simple cube of 5 x 5 x 5 mm, you can simply type:

```
cube([5,5,5]);
```

For the other functions such as the difference between two objects, you can look at the official documentation of the software at the following URL:

```
http://www.openscad.org/documentation.html
```

For the board I took as an example, I designed a simple case to hold the board still and included a hole for the external connections. It is basically made of the difference between two cube entities. I added another cube to make the hole on the side, and two cylinders to make the attaches for the board.

The following is one part of the case:

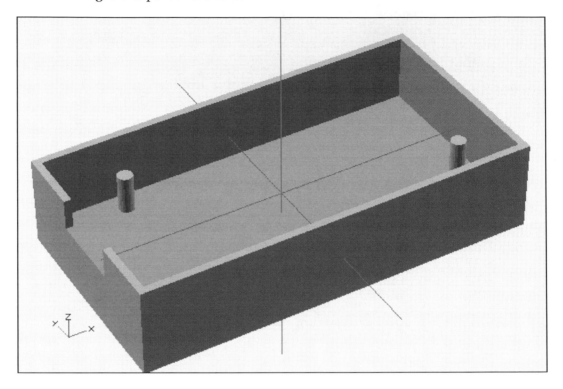

I also designed a cover to be able to close the case using the same principles. It is based on the union of two cube objects, so it fits nicely in the main part of the case.

The following is the result in OpenSCAD:

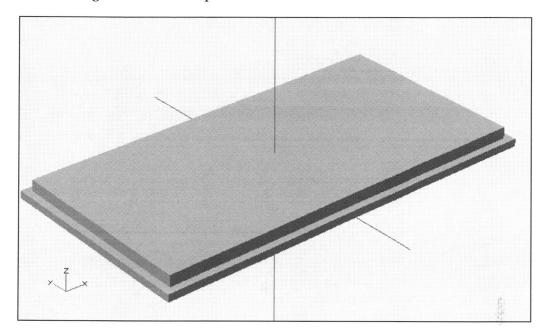

When your design is finished, you will have to export it to a special file format so that it can be 3D printed. To do so, go to **File** | **Export** and export the file as STL, which is the format required by many 3D printers and 3D-printing manufacturers.

The code for this part can be found inside the GitHub repository of the project at the following URL:

`https://github.com/openhomeautomation/arduino-home-automation/tree/master/chapter7`

Once your design is ready, you have to produce it. There are many ways to do this. Of course, one option is to print the case using your own 3D printer if you have one. If you don't, you will have to use one of the many 3D-printing services available on the Web.

I recommend using Shapeways. I don't have any commercial deal with them, it's just that their interface is very user-friendly and their prices are competitive. You can go to the following web address for more information:

```
https://www.shapeways.com/
```

You will be prompted to create an account and to upload your first file. The Shapeways interface will analyze the file and check whether it can be printed without potential problems. You will also get a price estimate for your design. The following is what I got with the case I uploaded:

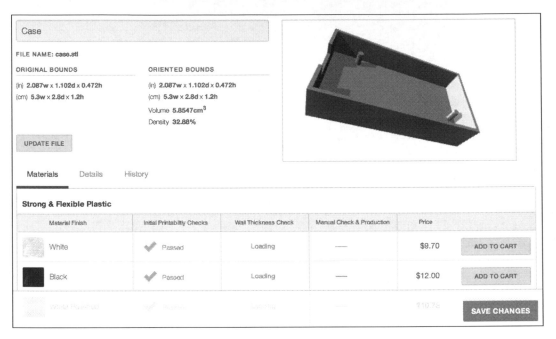

You can now choose your material and order; after a few weeks, you will receive your design. You can then assemble everything: the PCB, components, and 3D-printed case.

There are also other services you can use to 3D print your own case for the project. Another one I used is Sculpteo:

```
http://www.sculpteo.com/
```

You can also check out your local fab lab if there is one. They can usually print your designs for you at a much cheaper rate. To find out if there is one around where you live, check the official list at the following URL:

```
http://wiki.fablab.is/wiki/Portal:Labs
```

Summary

In this chapter, we saw how to build our own home automation system based on Arduino. We went through the three different stages of the process: prototyping your idea on a breadboard, designing and producing the PCB, and finally building a 3D-printed case for the project.

Let's have a look at the major takeaways from this chapter. First, we defined exactly what we wanted to achieve and chose the components for the project accordingly. As an example, we used a low-power Arduino system that is made to run on a battery.

Then, we built a prototype of this project on a breadboard, and literally built an Arduino system from scratch. We then also tackled the software part of the design by using a low-power library for Arduino.

After that step, we built a PCB based on the components we used for the breadboard prototype. We saw how to design a PCB and how to send it to a manufacturer in order to have it built for you. Finally, we saw the process of designing and building a 3D-printed case for your project.

As this is the end of the book, I want to summarize what we did in this book. We first saw the basics of home automation using the Arduino platform. We built wireless home automation projects based on Arduino using technologies such as XBee, Wi-Fi, and Bluetooth.

Then, we connected home automation projects to the Internet using a cloud service called Xively. This idea of connecting every object in your home to the Internet is called the *Internet of Things*, and I believe that in the future it will be a central element in any home automation system.

Finally, in the last two chapters of the book, we saw how to create our own home automation systems around Arduino, either by hacking existing devices or by creating your own device from scratch. Especially in this last chapter, I really wanted to show you the different steps that you can apply to any of your projects: prototyping with existing components, designing a board, manufacturing it, and finally producing a customized 3D-printed enclosure for your system.

I hope that the projects found in this book will give you the desire to go further and build even more projects to automate your home using the Arduino platform. The possibilities are nearly limitless, and I really encourage you to experiment and create your own designs based on what you learned in this book. Experiment, create, and most importantly, have fun doing it!

Index

R

relays
  about 22
  connecting, to power cables 26, 27
  controlling 32, 33
  testing 27-31
  URL, for information 22
REpresentational State Transfer (REST) 13

S

Sculpteo
  about 112
  URL 112
Seeedstudio 107
sensors
  URL 39
  URL, for working 68
Series 1 XBee module
  URL 8
Shapeways
  about 112
  URL 112
Software as a Service (SaaS) 13
SparkFun
  URL, for products 97

T

temperature measurement, with Bluetooth module project
  Arduino sketch, creating 44, 45
  hardware configuration 40-43
  hardware requisites 38-40
  humidity, measuring remotely 47-50
  humidity sensor, testing 46, 47
  software requisites 38-40
  temperature, measuring remotely 47-50
  temperature, testing 46, 47
TinyCircuits
  URL 83
TinyDuino processor board
  URL 84
TinyShield proto board
  URL 84
TinyShield USB & ICP
  URL 84

Tkinter module
  URL, for official documentation page 48

U

UART 14

W

Weather Station project
  about 53
  Arduino sketch, building 61-63
  components, connecting 55, 56
  data, displaying on Xively 64, 65
  hardware requisites 54
  logging in, on Xively 64
  sensors, testing 56, 58
  software requisites 54
Wi-Fi connection
  testing 27-31
Wireless XBee Motion Detectors
  hardware configuration 9-11
  hardware requisites 8, 9
  software requisites 8, 9

X

XBee explorer USB
  URL 8
XBee module 8
XBee motion detectors
  graphical interface, building for 15-18
  programming 13-15
Xively 53
Xively account
  setting up 58-61
Xively signup page
  URL 58

Z

ZigBee protocol 7

Thank you for buying
Arduino Home Automation Projects

About Packt Publishing

Packt, pronounced 'packed', published its first book "*Mastering phpMyAdmin for Effective MySQL Management*" in April 2004 and subsequently continued to specialize in publishing highly focused books on specific technologies and solutions.

Our books and publications share the experiences of your fellow IT professionals in adapting and customizing today's systems, applications, and frameworks. Our solution based books give you the knowledge and power to customize the software and technologies you're using to get the job done. Packt books are more specific and less general than the IT books you have seen in the past. Our unique business model allows us to bring you more focused information, giving you more of what you need to know, and less of what you don't.

Packt is a modern, yet unique publishing company, which focuses on producing quality, cutting-edge books for communities of developers, administrators, and newbies alike. For more information, please visit our website: www.packtpub.com.

About Packt Open Source

In 2010, Packt launched two new brands, Packt Open Source and Packt Enterprise, in order to continue its focus on specialization. This book is part of the Packt Open Source brand, home to books published on software built around Open Source licenses, and offering information to anybody from advanced developers to budding web designers. The Open Source brand also runs Packt's Open Source Royalty Scheme, by which Packt gives a royalty to each Open Source project about whose software a book is sold.

Writing for Packt

We welcome all inquiries from people who are interested in authoring. Book proposals should be sent to author@packtpub.com. If your book idea is still at an early stage and you would like to discuss it first before writing a formal book proposal, contact us; one of our commissioning editors will get in touch with you.

We're not just looking for published authors; if you have strong technical skills but no writing experience, our experienced editors can help you develop a writing career, or simply get some additional reward for your expertise.

C Programming for Arduino

ISBN: 978-1-84951-758-4   Paperback: 512 pages

Learn how to program and use Arduino boards with a series of engaging examples, illustrating each core concept

1. Use Arduino boards in your own electronic hardware and software projects.

2. Sense the world by using several sensory components with your Arduino boards.

3. Create tangible and reactive interfaces with your computer.

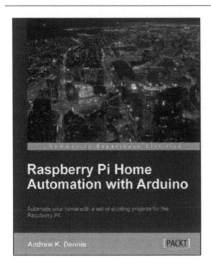

Raspberry Pi Home Automation with Arduino

ISBN: 978-1-84969-586-2   Paperback: 176 pages

Automate your home with a set of exciting projects for the Raspberry Pi!

1. Learn how to dynamically adjust your living environment with detailed step-by-step examples.

2. Discover how you can utilize the combined power of the Raspberry Pi and Arduino for your own projects.

3. Revolutionize the way you interact with your home on a daily basis.

Please check **www.PacktPub.com** for information on our titles

BeagleBone Robotic Projects

ISBN: 978-1-78355-932-9   Paperback: 244 pages

Create complex and exciting robotic projects with the BeagleBone Black

1. Get to grips with robotic systems.

2. Communicate with your robot and teach it to detect and respond to its environment.

3. Develop walking, rolling, swimming, and flying robots.

Internet of Things with the Arduino Yún

ISBN: 978-1-78328-800-7   Paperback: 112 pages

Projects to help you build a world of smarter things

1. Learn how to interface various sensors and actuators to the Arduino Yún and send this data in the cloud.

2. Explore the possibilities offered by the Internet of Things by using the Arduino Yún to upload measurements to Google Docs, upload pictures to Dropbox, and send live video streams to YouTube.

Please check **www.PacktPub.com** for information on our titles